LET'S DANCE

The Place of Dance in the Primary School

Kate Harrison

D0320155

Hodder & Stoughton

LONDON SYDNEY AUCKLAND

British Library Cataloguing in Publication Data

Harrison, Kate
　Let's Dance
　I. Title
　792.8

　ISBN 0-340-56497-0

First published 1993
Impression number　10　9　8　7　6　5　4　3　2　1
Year　　　　　　　　1998　1997　1996　1995　1994　1993

© 1993 Kate Harrison

All rights reserved. No part of this publication may be reproduced or transmitted in any form or by any means, electronic or mechanical, including photocopy, recording, or any information storage and retrieval system, without permission in writing from the publisher or under licence from the Copyright Licensing Agency Limited. Further details of such licences (for reprographic reproduction) may be obtained from the Copyright Licensing Agency Limited, of 90 Tottenham Court Road, London W1P 9HE.

Typeset by Wearset, Boldon, Tyne and Wear.
Printed in Great Britain for the educational publishing division of Hodder & Stoughton Ltd, Mill Road, Dunton Green, Sevenoaks, Kent TN13 2YA by Thomson Litho Ltd.

Contents

Acknowledgments

All the photographs and illustrations in *Let's Dance* have been taken from the classwork and choreography of Kate Harrison.

The author wishes to thank the following for their help:
the staff and pupils of Holy Trinity Primary School, London and Falmouth Community School; David Johnson, (London) and Broderick Ross, (Falmouth) for the photographs; Pat Hickman Jones, Dance Advisory Teacher for Cornwall.

The author and publishers would also like to thank the following for permission to use previously published material in *Let's Dance*. Chatto and Windus for the poem 'Lines' by Deborah Beswich from *That Way and This – Poetry for Creative Dance* and Macdonald and Evans for the poem 'Shadows' by Edith Stokes from *Word Pictures as a Stimulus for Creative Dance*.

Every effort has been made to trace copyright but if any copyright holders wish to contact Hodder and Stoughton they should do so at the publisher's address.

Dance is for all children in the primary school

Introduction

The *dance ideas* within this book are intended as an in-service resource to support schools and teachers with the introduction of dance as a foundation subject in the National Curriculum. Relevant theory, in limited form, has been offered where appropriate. The intention of the book has been to suggest and not dictate. Collectively, the text could be used as a simple, structured dance course, but ideally it will take teachers forward into making dances with their own children.

Teachers and schools will approach dance in the National Curriculum from many different perspectives. Some may already be reasonably confident and will only have to make minor adjustments to meet the new requirements. For others, the changes will be greater, especially for the generalist classroom teacher.

Dance is essentially a performing art. Its emotional power and visual impact cannot be contained in writing or communicated through reading. It is only through improvisation, composition and performance that the processes and content of the art of dance are properly understood.

> *'Primary teachers have two broad responsibilities in the arts. The first is to establish them, as soon as possible, as part of the daily habit of education. Young children have a natural interest and pleasure in movement and rhythm. . . . Second, the teacher must promote increasing confidence and competence in these activities.'*

('The Arts in Schools', Calouste Gulbenkian Foundation 1985)

The inclusion of dance within the National Curriculum has enormous benefits for all students within the state education system today:

► It allows all children, regardless of their class, colour, race or religion to have their chance to dance.

► Boys and girls will dance together giving an equal opportunity for all.

► Pupils and teachers will engage in the *making*, *presenting* and *responding* mode which is common to art work in a variety of media.

The use of dance in education allows us to explore our physical, emotional, spiritual and intellectual selves in an immediate, exciting and fulfilling way.

'The generalist teacher needs to have acquired sufficient knowledge through training and experience to understand the value of dance as part of a broad and balanced curriculum and to recognise and evaluate artistic quality in children's dance work.'

(P. Brinson 'Dance as Education', Falmer Press 1991)

There are many ways to explore dance with children and this book has been written to demonstrate some ways which will engage them in an accessible and enjoyable way.

Each chapter reflects and illuminates the *End of Key Stage Statements* and *Programmes of Study* for dance as set out in the National Curriculum document. Chapters 1 to 5 will help you to deliver the National Curriculum for dance effectively.

Most of us, teachers as well as children, need practical advice and some degree of success before we have the confidence and competence to allow ourselves and others total freedom in any art form. Dance is no exception and I make no apology for seeming somewhat prescriptive in places.

Remember, as you read on, that whatever stimulus or approach you use, enjoyment is at the heart of all learning: so do make sure that you, and all the children in your care, enjoy dancing together!

The rest of this section is devoted to the contents of the National Curriculum document with some necessary explanations and additions.

Dance within the National Curriculum
Dance is compulsory for pupils aged 5–11 in all state schools.

A Single Attainment Target
This should consist of statutory End of Key Stage Statements. The Attainment Target should encompass the planning and evaluating of activities, but the main emphasis should be on participation.

Programmes of Study
Dance is one of the six areas in PE which should be covered during Key Stages 1 and 2. The others are athletic activities, games, gymnastic activities, outdoor and adventurous activities and swimming.

End of Key Stage Statements
There are no 10-level statements of attainment in PE and dance. The End of Key Stage Statements represent the Attainment Target.

'The statutory framework for physical education is intended to allow schools and teachers wider discretion in teaching the subject than in the case of other National Curriculum subjects.'

(Physical Education in the National Curriculum, HMSO 1992)

The following End of Key Stage Statements and Programmes of Study are specific to dancework at Key Stages 1 and 2 and are taken from The Final Order:

KEY STAGE 1: END OF KEY STAGE STATEMENT AND PROGRAMMES OF STUDY (GENERAL)

End of Key Stage Statement	Programmes of Study	Non-Statutory Examples
Pupils should be able to show that they can:		
a) plan and perform a range of simple actions.	▶ develop a wide range of movements and activities.	jump, roll, run.
	▶ be encouraged to recognise and demonstrate.	
	▶ use movements to show moods and feelings and respond to simple rhythms and contrasting stimuli.	respond imaginatively to words, or other means of communication including music, poetry and stories as the stimulus to contrasting movement qualities.
	▶ learn to link movements to show change of direction or levels and variations of speed, tension or rhythm.	jump to roll to stand, travel and turn, skip in time.
b) practise and improve performance.	▶ be encouraged to practise and perform simple skills.	turning, jumping in different ways.
	▶ improve personal performance when working alone and, when ready, in co-operation with a partner.	show contrasting shapes whilst moving. leader/follower with a partner.

End of Key Stage Statement	Programmes of Study	Non-Statutory Examples

Pupils should be able to show that they can:

c) describe what they and others are doing.	▶ be given the opportunity to describe what they have done in dance, and how they did it, using simple terminology.	notice whether the movements are smooth or jerky; identify the difference between leaping and hopping; indicate that a dance was happy or sad.
d) recognise the effects of physical activities on their bodies.	▶ be made aware of the changes that happen to their bodies during exercise.	detect that heart beats faster, breathing rapid, body hotter during exercise.

KEY STAGE 2: END OF KEY STAGE STATEMENT AND PROGRAMMES OF STUDY (GENERAL)

End of Key Stage Statement	Programmes of Study (General)	Examples

Pupils should be able to show that they can:

a) plan, practise, improve, and remember more complex sequences of movement.	▶ be assisted to plan, refine and adapt performance when working with others.	improve, through practice, performance in a simple group dance.
	▶ develop, consolidate and combine physical skills through practice and rehearsal.	co-ordinate arm and leg actions.
	▶ remember, select and repeat a range of movements and perform more complex sequences alone and when working with others.	develop three movements into a sequence which can be repeated.

End of Key Stage Statement	Programmes of Study	Non-Statutory Examples
Pupils should be able to show that they can:		
b) perform effectively in activities requiring quick decision making.	▶ be encouraged to plan and use simple tactics and judge their success ▶ respond quickly to changing environments or adjust to other people's actions.	follow a partner matching or mirroring movements; adapt movements.
c) respond, alone and with others to challenging tasks, taking into account levels of skill and understanding.	▶ explore and present different responses to a variety of tasks and stimuli. ▶ work alone to ensure development of personal skills.	interpret the mood of a piece of music. be given time to develop a turning movement.
d) refers to swimming specifically.		
e) evaluate how well they and others perform and behave against criteria suggested by the teacher, and suggest ways of improving performance.	▶ help themselves to improve by making simple comments and judgements on their own and others' performance. ▶ be helped to understand their roles as members of groups and take into account others' ideas.	explain how they have performed the task; comment on the contrast shown in a phase of movement; suggest how to improve length and style in a jumping activity. judge how well individuals co-operate in a group task; take on the responsibilities of leader.

End of Key Stage Statement	Programmes of Study	Non-Statutory Examples

Pupils should be able to show that they can:

| f) sustain energetic activity over appropriate periods of time in a range of physical activities and understand the effects of exercise on the body. | ▶ understand the value of and demonstrate sustained activity over appropriate periods of time.

▶ understand the immediate and short term effects of exercise on the body.

▶ understand and demonstrate how to prepare for particular activities and to recover afterwards. | know and understand the reasons for changes in the pulse rate, breathing rate and body temperature during dance.

warm up for a specific activity; understand the necessity for time to recover from activity. |

The following dance expectations are stated in the *Programmes of Study (activity specific)* for dance:

Assessment is an ongoing process

Key Stage 1: Programmes of Study	Key Stage 2: Programmes of Study
Pupils should:	*Pupils should:*
► experience and develop control, co-ordination, balance, poise and elevation in basic actions including travelling, jumping, turning, gesture and stillness.	► be given opportunities to increase the range and complexity of body actions, step patterns and use of body parts.
► explore contrasts of speed, tension, continuity, shape, size, direction and level and describe what they have done.	► be guided to enrich their movements by varying shape, size, direction, level, speed, tension and continuity.
► experience working with a range and variety of contrasting stimuli, particularly music.	► in response to a range of stimuli express feelings, moods and ideas and create simple characters and narratives in movement.
► be given opportunities to explore moods and feelings through spontaneous responses and through structured tasks.	► make dances with clear beginnings, middles and ends involving improvising, exploring, selecting and refining content, and sometimes incorporating work from other aspects of the curriculum, in particular music, art and drama.
► be helped to develop rhythmic responses.	
► experience, and be guided towards making dances with clear beginnings, middles and ends.	► describe and interpret the different elements of a dance.

The learning processes in dance are not linear. All the dance expectations above are part of an ongoing process. They are intended to be used and reused many times during each Key Stage.

Assessment
The assessment should be as simple and straightforward as possible and should be based on the teacher's own judgements of pupils' performances. The assessment for dance should take place at or near the end of the Key Stage.

This assessment should not be based on one dance performance, but should be an ongoing process. The End of Key Stage Statements and the dance expectations contained in the Programmes of Study for Dance will help teachers to focus their attention on specific areas.

Special Educational Needs
Generally, there will be no new modifications or extra provisions for pupils with special educational needs.

Headteachers are allowed to give 'general directions' which exempt certain cases on a short term basis. All long term exceptions must have 'special directions' which should be applied sensitively and with regard to need to ensure a broad and balanced curriculum.

Wherever possible, all children regardless of their abilities and disabilities, will join together and dance.

Dance within the whole curriculum
Throughout the preparation stages and the final stages of the National Curriculum for Physical Education there has always been an acute awareness of the links which dance has with other curriculum areas. The working party for PE was instructed to work closely with Music and Drama colleagues. Dance is one of the first and most basic art forms. As dance is a performance art, many think that it should be a part of the Arts curriculum in schools. But dance is also very physical and is full of the

Movement as a means of expression and communication

participation and performance which is central to the single attainment target for PE

Wherever dance is placed in the curriculum it will flourish when taught with some expertise and a lot of enthusiasm. For instance, many primary school teachers include dancework in their topic-based approach to learning so that the children dance about a wide variety of ideas, subject areas and topics. Many of these are described in the *dance ideas* to be found throughout the text.

So let's move beyond the theory and ask ourselves what can realistically be achieved by the average seven and eleven year-old.

From four to seven years
These are active, energetic years when children enjoy all physical activities and delight in the joy of moving. These children are assertive, boisterous and physically confident. They need to move in a multitude of physically demanding ways and to use movement as a means of expression and communication.

In other words, typical four- to seven-year-olds need to dance! They need ongoing opportunities in the social atmosphere of school to accept new challenges, learn new skills and explore new images and ideas in action.

The teacher's role with children of this age is to provide exciting and challenging *dance ideas* which will help them to master their movements and develop new skills, so that their physical expressions become more satisfying to themselves and clearer for others to observe.

Between the ages of four and seven children gain awareness of what their bodies can do, where they can move and how actions are performed. They are also increasingly able to dance successfully with others.

From seven to eleven years
This is the time when the children are ready to move with increasing skill, co-ordination and control. It is also the time when the body becomes the dancer's instrument of expression. By the age of eleven all children who have experienced creative dance in school are able to communicate and express themselves freely through body language vocabulary.

Children change considerably both physically and emotionally between the ages of seven and eleven. At seven years many youngsters have entered into an 'ugly duckling' stage with missing teeth and changes in self-consciousness and body proportions. Bodies and bones change from now until adolescence. Rapid growth spurts lead to dramatic contrasts in height and weight and these (or the absence of them), often lead to inhibited physical and emotional responses. The teacher is able, through dance activities, to help overcome these inhibitions and to provide each child with a positive body awareness.

Body Talk
The art of dance has its own language – it's an expressive, communicative language without words: it's body talk!

Like all languages, dance has its own vocabulary which has to be systematically built up, revised, restructured and revisited. This vocabulary is outlined in the five chapters of this book:
Chapter 1 outlines the teacher's role and gives simple starting points. **(BASICS)**
Chapter 2 asks 'What can the body do?' **(ACTION)**
Chapter 3 explains 'Where the body can go.' **(SPACE)**
Chapter 4 looks at 'How the body moves.' **(DYNAMICS)**
Chapter 5 gets to the very heart of the National Curriculum by outlining the principles behind 'The Art of Making Dances.' **(FORM)**

There is no single way to introduce and teach creative movement and dance to children. Ideally, all the *dance ideas* in the book should be used as starting points.

Using the book

▶ Start by deciding which aspect of dancework to emphasise:

　　– the body in motion . . .
　　– spatial concepts . . .
　　– dance dynamics . . .
　　– dance compositions . . .

▶ Select a chapter, read through the opening section to the chapter then select an appropriate *dance idea*.

▶ Choose *Introductory Activities* (from Chapter 1) which will prepare the class for their dancework.

▶ Select and repeat element(s) of the *dance idea* and appropriate dance skills. Explore and improvise around these.

▶ Compose, perform and appraise even the simplest dance sequences. Consider and develop the material.

▶ Select suitable *Closing Activities* (from Chapter 1) to complete the cycle.

Let's look at some simple starting and finishing activities first.

Beginnings and endings

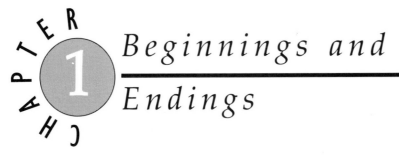

Beginnings and Endings

'Through making dances, however simple . . . primary school children can gain not only in physical knowledge and self confidence but also in experience of themselves in various contexts which would otherwise be denied them.'

(From 'Dance Education and Training in Britain', a nationwide survey carried out by the Calouste Gulkenkian Foundation 1985.)

So, how do you feel about getting children to create their own dances? Apprehensive? . . . Excited? . . . Terrified? . . . Fear not! Let's take one step at a time and ready, steady, slowly . . . go!

What to wear

Dancing is hot, hard work and too many clothes restrict whole body expressions.

The National Curriculum for PE states that pupils should:

▶ understand why particular clothing and protection are worn for different activities

▶ understand the dangers of wearing inappropriate dress and jewellery

▶ observe the rules of personal hygiene.

Ensure that the children are suitably dressed in PE or dance gear. You will sometimes be required to join in the action so try to dress appropriately too.

Shoes and trainers restrict the quality of dancework although soft shoes are recommended when the floor is old or dirty.

Musical resources

Children dance happily and creatively without any imposed musical accompaniment. Many dances are best performed in silence with natural body rhythms dictating the changes in the speed, strength and flow of action.

Often, dance activities are stimulated and/or accompanied by voice or body sounds. Others use a drum, tambourine or hand-held percussive instruments. This makes the activities accessible to busy classroom teachers.

In response to repeated requests by generalist teachers, all of the *dance ideas* in this book contain accompaniment suggestions. Some are pre-recorded and can be found through educational resource centres, local libraries, BBC Radio (movement and dance programmes) and reputable music shops. There is no right or 'finite' way to choose music for dance so, if you can, choose your own pieces.

The children are another invaluable musical resource. Do you have any musicians in your class? . . . A pianist? . . . Singers? . . . Percussion players? Use local talent within the school to stimulate and accompany dance activities.

One last musical note! There is an inherent relationship between music and movement. When music is used selectively it can allow the pupils to react with increased clarity and creativity. However, the human body has its own in-built rhythms and many, if not most, of the *dance ideas* in this book do not need any added accompaniment. Try to dance both in silence and in sound.

The teacher's role

Your energy, enthusiasm and participation are essential elements of successful dance sessions. So have a go, even if you feel very insecure at this stage. Remember that children are very sensitive to the attitude and involvement of adults. You alone can see how well the children understand and perform each activity. Only you can praise, encourage and comment on the quality of action.

The extent of your active participation depends on your observations and your assessment of the children's needs. Each and every group is unique and only you can judge when to join in and when to stand back.

Always ask for dancework of a high standard and be ready to repeat and revise new material and old favourites. Tell the children if they can do better and show examples of quality work regularly.

The quest for quality in dance is more easily observed than defined in words. It can be a simple action such as a jump which explodes off the floor and seems to hover in mid air, or a balance which seems to stretch and grow endlessly.

The learning process

The principles of dance are inter-relating threads which appear in all 'educationally sound' dance lessons:

- Performing
- Composing
- Appreciating

The Physical Education Working Party and the National Curriculum Council have placed the emphasis on *performance*.

Pupils should:

▶ be *physically active* in physical education lessons

▶ be encouraged to demonstrate knowledge and understanding mainly through *physical actions* rather than verbal explanations

▶ learn and consolidate particular skills through *practice and repetition*

▶ learn to *evaluate* their initial attempts

▶ be encouraged to use *terminology* relevant to the activities undertaken.

The method

▶ Introductory Activities – are designed to bring the group together as a cohesive unit, to warm up bodies and minds, to introduce relevant dance techniques and skills and to establish concentrated physical participation.

▶ Dance Developments – allow for explorations of the initial *dance idea*, consideration of the dance skills which are required and the composition of the final dance form.

This section is the main part of every lesson and is much more than a compilation of skilful movements. It involves the selection of appropriate movements which express and communicate a particular idea or image. This is a process of selection, rejection, improvisation and shaping.

▶ Quiet Endings – is the time to take stock and to put an incomplete *dance idea* on hold until next time. Calm, closing activities are essential, especially at Key Stages 1 and 2, because they precede other equally important activities within the school day.

The rest of this chapter is devoted to *Starting* and *Finishing* activities. Most of the introductory activities can be adapted to form *Finishing Ideas* and *Quiet Endings*.

So, now you're ready . . .

Let's get steady! . . . and ready? Steady? – Off you go!

Off you go!

Introductory Activities

You can perform almost every one of these activities without music. You can clap, tap, slap, beat or shake out the rhythms.

From the very start, encourage the children to move every part of their bodies. Begin with fingers and see how they bend, stretch, twist and turn. Flex and rotate the wrists. See what the elbows, shoulders, knees and hips can do. The human body is not nearly as limited as you think!

Make the introductory activities seem like games, even if they involve hard technical dancework. Their aim is initially to free the children of self-consciousness and shyness and to concentrate their minds and bodies. Some are more suitable for older and some for younger children, but use age categories with caution and flexibility. Confident five year-olds may accomplish with ease what less experienced seven year-olds have spent weeks learning. Eleven year-olds who have developed many successful dances often enjoy simple starting games as much as five year-olds do! The children will request the 'starters' which they like best again and again. Don't be afraid to repeat them. You can make each version different from the time before.

Dance is a process of discovery, improvisation, invention and creation. These activities are springboards to the world of dance. They open up the excitement of tangling with gravity and travelling through space in a multitude of marvellous moving ways!

Rhythm games

Find your own beat	Take your own pulse using wrist and fingers. Tap a foot in time to the pulse. Walk, then run and see what happens. Try moving in and out of each other with individual pulse rate patterns.
Walk – run – gallop	Practise moving to a walking, a running and a galloping rhythm. Then play the rhythms in different orders to form a listening then moving activity. Make it more difficult by introducing backwards and turning movements.
Drumbeats	The American Indians and African drummers have been doing it for centuries – the possibilities are endless: pass messages by passing sounds around a circle, rubbing hands, clicks, claps, thigh slaps, stamps, words and whispers. Create movements to accompany these sounds.
The mirror game	As a class group facing you or in pairs – sitting, kneeling, standing or moving sideways. Use isolated body parts then shrinking and growing activities.
Sculptor and clay	In pairs. The sculptor moulds the clay into curled, stretched and twisted shapes. Explore balancing, spinning, swaying. Each action should lead to the next to form a repeatable sequence.
Listen and move	Start on the floor with eyes shut. Listen to the sound of an instrument or some music and respond in movement. Ask the children to use their bodies to describe in movement the sound of a gong . . . Indian bells . . . wood blocks . . . maracas . . . a bamboo flute . . . finger cymbals . . . a tambour drum. Point out that stillness is being alert and intent and ready for the next sound.

Run, run, run!	Run in a circle
	Run in a hurry
	Run in slow motion
	Run backwards
	Run and fly
	Run and spin
	Run and spiral
	Run and shrink
	Run and grow
	Run and stop and run. Stop!
	Also try running like animals, insects, clowns, monsters, thieves, cartoon characters . . . This activity can be repeated using other travelling actions.

Follow-my-leader ideas

| Follow-my-leader class lines | Lead the class out of the circle into a follow-my-leader class line with slow, tip-toeing actions. Then march your line round and round the room. Stop, and leave the line so that the child behind you becomes the new leader. |

Follow my teacher

The new leader chooses another travelling activity such as skipping, hopping, jumping, trotting or galloping, and you clap or play the appropriate rhythm for this. Change leaders frequently, and encourage as many new ways of travelling as possible. Older children can copy movement combinations such as hopping and jumping, and can change from high to low levels as they move along the line.

The follow-my-leader line can become a giant centipede with wide-stepping feet and stretched, wiggling arms; a mighty monster with the children plodding in unison; a train shuffling round and round with elbow wheels; or a circus parade with clowns, animals and colourful characters leading the action.

Follow-my-leader pairs   Play follow-my-leader footprints. The followers have to step exactly in the footprints of the person in front. This game can be made more challenging by increasing or decreasing the size, speed or strength of the actions, adding appropriate arm gestures, or combining steps, jumps and hops to make stepping patterns.

Group lines   Follow-my-leader lines can be in twos, threes, small or large groups. Divide the class into two lines, then march both lines together towards you at one end of the hall. Stop the marching with the word 'HALT!' then ask the children to 'about turn' so that the last becomes first and the child who was at the back of the line is now the new leader. With practice, these two lines will be able to march around the room in opposite directions, to make circles and to follow figure-of-eight floor patterns.

Try the following in lines and circles:

Circles dancing

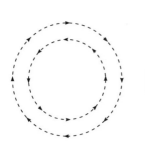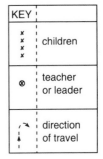

KEY	
x x x x	children
⊗	teacher or leader
↗ ↑	direction of travel

Dance formations

Quiet Endings

A reflective, relaxing transition period:

The name game	touching each child in turn, saying goodbye. Each child quietly says their name then tiptoes to the door until one class line has been formed.
Listening and moving	play a suitable piece of music or recite a poem or a short story then ask the children to move together during and at the end of the story.
Follow-my-leader Rhythm games Circle games	Adapt and repeat some of the introductory activities.
Drumbeat	Eyes closed. One person walks amongst the group and bangs the drum from different places. Focus with the body and make gestures towards the drumbeat.
Rag dolls	Breathe in slowly with arms raised until touching above head. Hold breath, then breathe out quickly bringing arms to side again and letting the whole body go floppy.
Knees, elbows, heads and toes	Lie full length on backs, hands by sides, eyes shut, quiet! Think about your toes, don't move anything else. Wriggle your toes, stretch your toes – relax them. Now do the same with your ankles, knees, hips, shoulders, elbows, head and fingers. Stress the relaxation and discover who in the group finds this difficult.
Trapped!	An on the spot activity which explores the 'personal' space around the body. Experiment with being caught in a large glass bottle, a giant spider web, a balloon, and a tub of something very sticky.
Isolations	On a loud drumbeat the movement must be tense, abrupt and focused. The 'freeze' is held until the next beat. On a soft beat the body is relaxed so that, although the feet stay in position, the head, shoulders,

	elbows, wrists and waist all swing freely.
Tightropes	There is a tightrope stretched out in front of you. It is about six feet from the ground. Step along using arms to balance and pauses. Sway, swing, flop and wobble. Finally, find your own point of balance and repeat the whole exercise.
Sounds like . . .	Eyes closed. Listen. Sort out the sounds you hear from outside – the street, playground, farm, sea, traffic. When the drum bangs, cut out these sounds and listen to the sounds inside the room. React appropriately in movement to the sounds outside and inside the room. Change when the drum beats.

A last word

The *starters* and *endings* in this chapter should not be used in 'recipe' fashion but as the beginnings and endings of *dance ideas*.

When choosing introductory activities or quiet endings to lessons, try to make sure that they are, in some way, related to the chosen *dance idea*.

Some starters may even make excellent endings in certain situations. Play it by ear, choose your own structure and enjoy starting to dance together!

Beginnings and endings

Body action

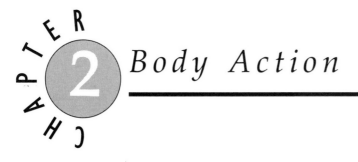

2 Body Action

Creative dance for the child and the teacher starts from known, everyday activities such as running, skipping, leaping, turning, falling and balancing.

The National Curriculum for Dance states that at Key Stage 1, pupils should:

experience and develop control, co-ordination, balance, poise and elevation in basic actions including travelling, jumping, turning, gesture and stillness.

The same range of whole body actions apply to Key Stage 2, but by this stage the pupils should:

be given opportunities to increase the range and complexity of body actions, step patterns and use of body parts.

The initial aim of the teacher is to enable the children to enjoy moving with confidence and without inhibitions. This is achieved by starting with familiar movements within a secure, controlled environment.

The early lessons are concerned with 'the body in action' and the discovery of 'what the body can do'. This chapter covers, through a selection of varied and contrasting *dance ideas*:

▶ Movement of the whole body – bending, stretching and twisting. Travelling, turning, elevation, gesture and weight transference (the five basic body activities).

▶ Body parts – loosening, leading, contracting, isolating, accompanying.

▶ Motion and stillness.

The priority throughout is to provide *dance ideas* which make high physical demands on the children in an exciting and enjoyable way.

'We have found that one of the first stages in gaining interest and respect for dance has been the recognition that it can be physically demanding.'

(*Creative Dance for Boys*. Peter Lofthouse. Jean Carroll.)

Dance is physically demanding

Into Action

KEY STAGE 1

Accompaniment: *Find your favourite thing to do* – an action rhyme.

'Can you run and can you stop?
Can you stay still on one spot?
You can tiptoe toe to toe.
Ready, steady, slowly go!
Can you balance? Well, let's see . . .
On one leg or on one knee?
Can you spin yourself around?
Now you're sinking to the ground.
Jump up quickly all of you . . .
And find your favourite thing to do!'

Tiptoe toe to toe

The action rhyme above contains the following body actions – run, stop, tiptoe, balance, spin and sink.

Spend time on each section of the rhyme and do not rush from one activity to the next.

▶ Use the questioning tone of the poem to ask the children to improve the quality of their performance, and to show good examples of dancework to the rest of the class.

▶ Encourage variety, by asking for changes of level and contrasting directions.

▶ Spend time improvising whenever possible. There are many ways to run – quickly, slowly, directly and indirectly, lightly and strongly. There are also many more ways to balance than merely on one leg or one knee. Experiment and encourage new ways whenever possible.

▶ Younger children will need your guidance to form a sequence of movement which can be repeated and re-visited over a number of movement sessions.

▶ Older children will enjoy the challenges and questions and will soon become familiar with the whole rhyme. Ask them to perform and revise the given format from week to week, then to invent their own action rhymes.

KEY STAGE 2
Accompaniment: Action words

Create a dance from the following action words:

Travel/turn
Curl/stretch
Fall/rise.

▶ Keep the sequence order but improvise on the numerous different ways of travelling, turning, opening, closing, sinking and rising.

▶ Add changes in speed and strength.

▶ Add changes in level and direction.

▶ Work in pairs in unison, then one after the other as leader and follower or as part of an action and reaction dance.

▶ Explore the following phrases using basic body activities:
Turning – curling, writhing, twisting and unfolding.
Curling, Stretching and Jumping – expand, contract, explode, cascade.
Jumping – jumping here, jumping there, jumping, jumping everywhere.

Rising, Falling and Turning – round and round, up and down, sink and roll away.

▶ Find new words to describe the basic body activities – travel, turn, jump, gesture, weight transference.

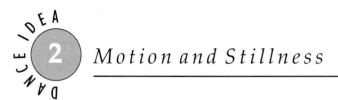

Motion and Stillness

KEY STAGE 1

Accompaniment: Going and stopping phrases

> Run and freeze
> Creep and wait
> March and halt!
> Stand up straight.

Use this action rhyme to explore travelling and stopping in different ways.

▶ Talk about and move like a variety of 'things that go' and 'things that stop'. Include animals, insects, machines, toys, weather, in your explorations.

▶ Play a 'musical statues' type game with the emphasis on stopping in different ways. Ask for a freeze, a balance, a wobble and a fall. Tell the children how you expect them to stop before they start each running phrase, e.g. 'Run and stop, and fall! Run and stop, and wobble! Run and freeze! Run and stop, and balance!'

▶ Vary the travelling activity as well as the stopping action. Older children can create their own short going and stopping dances in pairs.

▶ Use these moving and stopping words to form simple dance phrases:

Travelling words				*Stopping and balancing words*		
trot	stamp	skip	scurry	settle	freeze	stop
step	march	gallop	tiptoe	hover	perch	wobble
stride	creep	crawl	walk	hold	linger	pause
run	slither	jump	slide	stay		rest

Every action can be performed in numerous different ways and the children can be challenged to vary the speed, strength, shape and size of their actions.

Going and stopping

KEY STAGE 2
Accompaniment: Going and stopping words

▶ Work out phrases of running and stopping using some of the following 'stopping and balancing words'.

wait	settle	freeze	stop	collapse	hover
hold	perch	pause	wobble	stay	linger

▶ Find different ways to travel using some of the 'travelling words' listed below. Try to combine an appropriate stopping action with your chosen method of travelling:

step	trot	creep	gallop	tiptoe
skip	stride	march	walk	scurry
run	slither	crawl	jump	slide

Enjoying dancing

Create a short dance based on travelling and stopping in numerous
different ways:

▶ emphasise the contrasts between speed, level, shape, strength, for
example, suddenly freezing or slowly settling; hovering high or
collapsing low

▶ create a 'surprise' dance with one or more people based on the use of
stillness and the unpredictability of going and stopping activities

▶ try using different body activities to arrest the action, for example,
jump – spin – stamp – sink – spiral – fall

▶ follow each action with immediate stillness.

In pairs, improvise around the images created by the phrases 'Things that
stop' and 'Things that go'. Ask each pair to concentrate on one image
only, for example, transport, a washing machine, an animal, an insect, an
athlete, cartoon characters and to concentrate on the way that they go,
and the way that they stop.

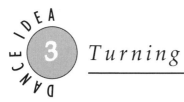

③ *Turning*

KEY STAGE 1

Accompaniment: *Turning here, turning there* – an action rhyme

'Turning here, turning there
Turning, turning everywhere.
I can spin and I can stop
See me balance, twist and hop!
One last turn to finish, so . . .
Whirl up high and spin down low.'

Use the poem above to create a dance with the words as the stimulus and accompaniment for action:

▶ contrast turning slowly and quickly

▶ add a jump, a change of level, a gesture or a change of strength to the turn

▶ combine travelling and turning

▶ think about 'things that turn' and select a few examples to move about, for example, wheels, circles, clocks, balls, cotton bobbins unravelling.

Things that turn

Accompaniment: Action words and phrases

▶ Use the following words to create a dance based on turning:

                    whirl   whip
        twirl   spin   roll
spiral   swirl   curl   twist

and intersperse the turning words above with these gesturing words:

reach   scatter   dab
        stretch   gather
grab   touch   punch
        press   kick

▶ Now form phrases of movement from both the turning and gesturing words:

> Stretch/curl/roll/grab
> Gather/swirl/spiral/scatter
> Kick/curl/roll/reach

▶ use images such as a wheel, a cotton bobbin, a cassette tape and a whirlwind to demonstrate turning on and off the spot

▶ practise turning in pairs quickly and slowly; lightly and strongly

▶ create new combinations, for example, turn and travel, turn and jump, turn and gesture, turn and spiral

▶ use traditional and country dance forms as the stimulus for turning actions

▶ introduce circle dances. Use hoops and ribbons as extra stimuli for dances involving turning.

4 *Jumping*

Accompaniment: *Jumping here, jumping there . . .* an action rhyme

'Jumping here, jumping there
Jumping, jumping everywhere!

I can bounce and I can hop!
See me run, and see me stop!
One last jump to finish, so
Leap up high and jump down low.'

▶ Contrast bouncing on the spot with feet together, with jumping freely in a variety of body shapes (for example, stretched, spiky), and directions (for example, forwards, backwards and sideways):

▶ combine hopping and jumping to form a 'hopscotch' pattern

▶ explore jumping with feet apart and feet together, then try hopping and balancing in wide shapes

▶ combine running and stopping to form phrases of action, at different levels

▶ use the phrase 'things that jump' to stimulate numerous different jumping actions, for example, animals, insects, toys and machines.

KEY STAGE 2
Accompaniment: Word and voice sounds

There are five basic jumps:
From one foot to the same foot
From one foot to the other foot
From one foot to both feet
From both feet to both feet
From both feet to one foot.

Try out each jump, then combine travelling and jumping in different ways.

▶ Create a sequence using all five jumps, not just once but a number of times. Vary the order. Be as inventive as possible.

▶ Take the following words:

Jumping

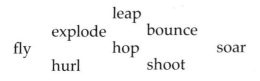

and improvise movements using these words ensuring that the emphasis is on elevation and leaving the floor.

▶ Choose three words to form short sequences of action, for example,

> hop/bounce/leap
> explode/fly/bounce

Add some slow turning words, for example, swirl, whirl and curl to complete and augment the action: curl – explode – fly – swirl – whirl – bounce.

▶ Use 'flight' as the stimulus and the words fly – soar – swirl – whirl – glide to create a dance with the theme of 'Birds in flight'.

▶ Explore numerous different 'Things that jump!'

▶ Create a dance using the following combinations: gesture and turn/ hop and jump/turn and jump/jump and freeze.

▶ Discover more about elevation through improvisation around 'Things that rise and sink' and 'Things that fly!'.

Games and sport

Games we play

KEY STAGE 1
Accompaniment: Playground chants, nursery rhymes and songs

Stopping and starting games	Try 'Musical Statues', 'What's the time Mr Wolf?', 'Grandmother's Footsteps' and 'Tag'. These should be controlled through exaggerated stopping points.
Follow my leader lines	Lead the class initially, then choose one child to lead a follow-my-leader line around the room. Develop by changing leaders and activities frequently, for example, skipping then stopping then jumping, jumping and clapping, galloping.
Dancing in lines, circles and figures of eight	Lead the line around the room then make circles which skip clockwise. Try skipping in one huge figure of eight pattern. Try this with the class divided into two groups and eventually form two concentric circles. Older age groups can perform the above activities in small groups with changes of leader.

Here we go round the mulberry bush	A circle skipping game. When the children reach the words 'this is the way' all sorts of shapes, sizes and action ideas can be introduced such as clapping, jumping, rising, shrinking, stamping, turning, balancing. Ask for ideas from the group and encourage a response with actions not words.
Circle games	Try 'Ring-a-Ring o' Roses', 'Silly Old Mulligan Lost His Hat', 'We All Clap Hands Together' and the 'Hokey Cokey'.
Hopscotch	Alone, or in pairs, the children work through the step/jump combinations. Clap the rhythm.
Quiet endings	You are leader and the class curls up in spaces on the ground. Touch each child gently in turn, then they must stand without a sound and tiptoe along behind you. When the line is complete, finish the session by leading the children out of the movement area. Eventually, the children will be able to lead and perform this activity without your participation.

Super sports

KEY STAGE 1
Accompaniment: *Match of the Day*, *Grandstand* and similar TV themes

Sports statues	Running and stopping in sports shapes. Stress the need for sudden, clear statue stops and quick changes in direction.
Famous photos	Develop each 'stopping and starting' phrase as if really playing a sport, for example, dodging, darting, hitting, throwing. Make the movements larger than life and at the end of each phrase freeze in a clear statue shape 'as if someone's taken your photograph'.
Slow motion replays	Introduce slow motion to clarify and exaggerate the action further, for example, a tennis serve (reach, hit and run), putting the shot (stretch, spin and throw), a football goal (run and kick, run and jump).
A sports dance	Choose dances using the above ideas in pairs with the emphasis on stopping and starting,

Sports statues

changes in speed, and introducing the idea of action and reaction.

Sports day — Concentrate on athletic events such as running, jumping, throwing. Again, create phrases and 'photo finishes' and when every child has a phrase ask for leaders who are willing to demonstrate, so that the class group can follow and learn new phrases of action. Create phrases containing jumps, falls, rolls, statues, twists and bends.

An obstacle course — In groups, using props such as hoops, ropes and benches, create short dances which highlight the words 'over', 'under', 'around', 'along' and 'through'. The obstacles should be a mixture of people and props and each child should participate in the obstacle course.

The victory dance — A rhythmic skipping, running and clapping dance around and around the room, waving like sports superstars.

5 Cats

KEY STAGE 1
Accompaniment: Word and voice sounds

Stretching and curling into cat shapes, curl, arch or stretch from low shapes on the floor to wide, outstretched shapes on hands and feet, or high on tiptoes:

▶ isolate the paws and claws by suddenly popping each finger out of a fist in turn. Try extending and curling toes as the legs lazily stretch and curl

▶ form phrases of creeping and stopping, then creeping and leaping. Emphasise the long stretched leaps which break up the creeping

▶ form a short dance about cats using this action rhyme:

'Quiet creeping
Curling, rolling
Leap and twirl away.'

▶ older children will be able to dance in pairs sometimes at the same time and sometimes one after the other.

KEY STAGE 2
Accompaniment: Music from *Cats* by Andrew Lloyd Webber – Voice sounds

Introduce the idea of cats as a stimulus for a dance using combinations of crouching, stretching, stalking, pouncing and curling actions:

▶ develop an action/reaction dance sequence between two squabbling cats: create changes in speed, level and direction

▶ introduce a prop, such as a dustbin, for the cats to hide behind, move in and out of, creep around, and appear above and below it

▶ improvise in groups accompanied by voice sounds to represent cats meeting together: contrast creeping slowly with fast running; sudden pouncing with stillness; fast turning with slow sinking; rolling and curling with stretching

▶ play games of follow-my-leader cats, changing leaders and step patterns frequently: finish with a 'heads and tails' game with the cats chasing their tails

▶ create a shadow dance based on 'Night-time cats'.

Cats

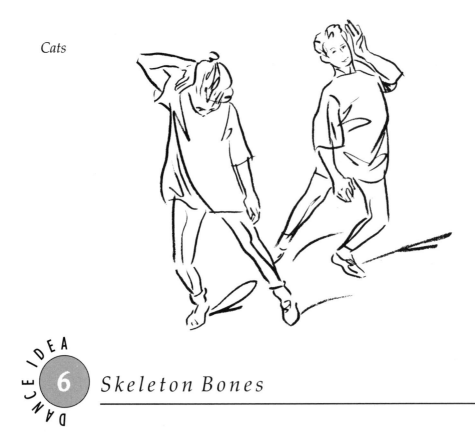

Skeleton Bones

KEY STAGE 1
Accompaniment: Chopin's *Black Key Study*

Make skeleton shapes with bony arms, loose limp shoulders, knocking knees, nodding heads and floppy fingers. Dance isolated parts of the body in turn:

▶ practise growing into skeleton shapes then collapsing one body part at a time, for example, heads then knees, then hands, shoulders and finally the torso

▶ create a jerky jolting skeleton dance, hopping from foot to foot

▶ add sudden statue stops to ensure the clarity of the body shape

▶ create a follow-my-leader skeleton dance in pairs, then in a class line

▶ make a whole class skeleton with groups of children as the head, arms, legs, fingers, torso. Then move these 'body parts' in isolation and then all at the same time

▶ take a trip through the Ghost Train with skeletons, spider webs, ghosts and strange noises!

Skeleton bones

KEY STAGE 2

Accompaniment: *Fossils* from *The Carnival of the Animals* by Saint-Saens

Create a jerky dance where joints of the legs and arms lead. Include motion and stillness, jumps, falls and gestures:

▶ find appropriate voice and body sounds, for example, slap, tap, click, to accompany the action

- with a partner, put the two solo dances together as a skeleton duet. Adapt the movement and sound accordingly to develop the relationship that evolves

- create a movement conversation between the two skeletons with isolated body parts dominating, for example, fingers flopping, heads nodding, knees knocking

- form group lines maintaining skeleton shapes. Try a 'domino effect' collapse of the skeletons

- consider making a dance in three sections – A B C; C culminating in the domino effect of falling skeletons!

- create a dance drama around Ahlberg's *Funny Bones*

- make up a song and dance routine accompanied by *Dry Bones*, a traditional West Indian song.

 **7** *Clowns*

KEY STAGE 1
Accompaniment: *The Golliwog's Cakewalk* by Debussy

Explore walking in different ways – on toes, heels, sides of feet:

- let the children explore their own ideas for walking in different ways. Emphasise the clown's long, flat shoes which will require high knees, wide-apart feet, walking with toes in the air or with feet turned inwards or outwards

- vary the height of the walk

- introduce a wibbly-wobbly quality by suggesting that the clown sometimes overbalances and almost falls

- finish with a sudden fall, followed by kicking legs high into the air

- in pairs, create a 'custard pie' routine with stretching, throwing and falling actions, ducking and diving, then *slowly* scraping the mixture off faces

▶ practise and develop other clown routines, for example, ducking to dodge one end of a ladder only to get knocked flat by the other end; getting a foot or a head stuck in any imaginary bucket

▶ create cartoons, circuses, carnival parades, fancy dress parties and celebrations featuring clowns.

Clowns

Accompaniment: Scott Joplin's *Pineapple Rag*

Work on the stereotype clown with flat, flapping feet, stretched fingers and funny face. Spend time exploring lots of different 'funny' ways of walking. Look for contrasting shapes, exaggerated actions and the maintenance of clear body shapes and facial expressions:

▶ use a class follow-my-leader line to allow several different clowns to lead the line in a variety of funny ways

▶ differentiate between sensible clowns and silly clowns. The sensible clowns adopt an upright posture with their noses held high in the air. The silly clowns, in contrast, fall and roll, tripping over their own flat feet

▶ form 'silly' and 'sensible' pair routines. Work on balance and off balance and include 'action/reaction' routines

▶ introduce 'talented' clowns who balance in different shapes, cartwheel, leap and perform amazing athletic routines. Form pair routines where the 'silly' clown tries to mimic the acrobatics of the talented clowns

▶ use props to add variety to the clown routines, for example, hoops to move through, benches to balance on, mats for cartwheels, buckets, balloons, feather dusters, ladders

▶ explore lots of funny ways of walking 'Monty Python' style

▶ create a silent movie in 'Charlie Chaplin' style.

3 *All Sorts of Shapes and Sizes*

All sorts of shapes and sizes

This chapter is all about using the space around us and discovering 'where the body can go'.

At Key Stage 1 the National Curriculum expects seven-year-olds to:

explore contrasts of speed, tension, continuity, shape, size, direction and level and describe what they have done.

The same spatial concepts occur in the Programmes of Study for Key Stage 2 in that pupils should:

> *be guided to enrich their movements by varying shape, size, direction, level, speed, tension and continuity and describe the expressive features of dance.*

Two statements which might, on the surface, appear to be very similar. The *dance ideas* in this chapter show clearly how much more can be expected of and achieved by the eleven year-old in comparison to the seven year-old. They also show the development, repetition and cross-referencing which occurs between the two Key Stages.

Finding space

The ability to find space is a skill that can be taught. It is very often assumed that finding space happens naturally. It does not! It is easily learned and it is easily forgotten. The luxury of being the only one in a dance space is something children learning to dance rarely experience.

Finding spaces must be an integral part of every session. Remember that the words 'spread out' do not have the same meaning as 'find yourself a space'. There are many more 'spacing' tips later in the chapter.

On the spot and into spaces

The space around us can be divided into two categories. These are:

personal space – which can be thought of as a huge balloon which extends as far as the body can reach without moving off the spot

general space – which involves orientation in the whole room area.

Children at Key Stages 1 and 2 should have plenty of opportunities to move on the spot as well as in the whole room space.

Spatial areas

The most simple and easily understood are the three levels of movement – high, medium and deep. The high level is bordered by the ceiling, the deep level by the floor and the medium level is bordered by the walls.

Other spatial concepts such as over, under, around, below, into and out of are highlighted within this chapter, as are improvisations around the three dimensions of height, width and depth: forwards and backwards; side and side; up and down.

Shapes and sizes

Children use their bodies in any manner of inventive ways to describe all sorts of contrasting shapes and sizes.

There are four basic shapes which can be made with a human body – the arrow, the wall, the ball and the screw shape. These shapes arise out of the fact that the body can bend, stretch and twist. All other body shapes are variations of these movements.

The 'arrow' is one dimensional and pierces the space. The 'wall' is two dimensional and stretches and spreads sideways. The 'ball' and the 'screw' are three dimensional with the spine curving and twisting.

The body can bend, stretch and twist

All these shapes and all the variations on the shapes, can be made to travel, leap, turn, contract, expand and freeze. The size of movement is another important factor because it allows the dancer to perform with varying degrees of extension and contraction.

These, and the other ideas about changing levels, directions, shapes and sizes are just the beginning of a whole host of exciting explorations into the world around us.

Finding Spaces

Statue games

KEY STAGE 1
Accompaniment: Nursery songs and rhymes; skipping rhythms

Practise moving from space to space without colliding. Start with a game of tiptoe statues. Ask for silent tiptoeing in and out of everyone else. Then children 'freeze' every time you clap your hands. There are no winners or losers, just praise for quick reactions and good spacing:

▶ play 'musical bumps', where the children stop on cue and fall to the floor: it is easier to point out good spacing when the class is seated

▶ play 'musical statues' with the children skipping in and out of spaces, then 'freezing' when the music stops

Marching with the soldiers

▶ bring the statue shapes to life by using contrasting travelling activities, for example, bouncing like a ball, trotting like a horse, marching with the soldiers: then stop the action with appropriate stopping words, such as 'Whoa!' and 'Halt!'

▶ use nursery rhymes such as *Wee Willie Winkie* for spacing games and to introduce changes in the level of action:

'Wee, Willie Winkie runs through the town (PAUSE)
Upstairs and downstairs in his night-gown (PAUSE)
Tapping at the window (PAUSE)
Crying through the lock (PAUSE)
"Are all the children in their beds? It's past 8 o'clock." '

Famous photos

KEY STAGE 2
Accompaniment: TV and film themes

▶ Play musical statues with the emphasis on staying still for a photograph on each statue stop.

▶ Choose a cartoon character and move 'in role', in and out of spaces, stopping for photographs when the music stops. For example, *Donald Duck* with flat, flappy feet; cartoon cat with high spiky knees.

▶ Try moving in different directions, sometimes forwards, sometimes backwards and sideways.

▶ Bring photographs from magazines and newspapers as the stimulus for action.

▶ Work in pairs to create a series of 'photographs' about a famous couple, for example, royalty, sports personalities, politicians, TV and film stars. Emphasise moving into and out of the still photo shapes. Create phrases of action which lead up to each photograph.

▶ Create a story around one or more photographs. Create a dance about this story. Make sure that the dance uses lots of room space, that it contains statue stops in spaces and that it has a clear beginning, middle and ending.

▶ Use props such as elastic, hoops and ropes to help the pupils to gain spatial awareness.

On the spot and into spaces

Bubbles and balloons

KEY STAGE 1
Accompaniment: Voice sounds and silence

Bubbles and balloons effectively demonstrate how shapes change with movement on the spot and into a space.

Blow up a variety of balloon shapes. Ask the children to observe the changes in shape and size and to interpret these shapes with their whole bodies:

▶ grow into each of the balloon shapes – round, twisted or thin

▶ use bubbles to show how balloons and bubbles rise, drift and float through the air

▶ ask the children to use whole body movements to show how the bubble travels and turns, rises and sinks, turns and swirls

▶ use jumps, hops, falls and rolls to show how the bubble bursts

Balloon shapes

▶ let the air out of an inflated balloon to show what happens when air is suddenly released. Encourage whizzing, whirling, jumping, leaping, turning, spiralling actions

▶ 'Pop!' This is the sudden ending to a sequence where the balloon is blown up, floats through the air and bursts. Make clear distinctions between movement on the spot and movement into spaces.

The birth bubble

KEY STAGE 2
Accompaniment: *'Gymnopedie 1 and 3'* Satie/Debussy.

The emphasis at this stage is being on the inside growing outwards. The balloon, the bubble or the egg is the personal space around the body.

Use a stretchy, elastic balloon to demonstrate growing bigger and bigger bit by bit. Ask the children to grow using their whole bodies as you blow up the balloon:

▶ try reaching forwards, backwards, sideways, upwards and downwards as though inside a huge, stretchy balloon

▶ introduce the idea of chicks hatching from eggs to encourage the children to emerge from the bubble using varied body parts to push, pull, reach, stab and eventually burst out

▶ spend time practising 'balance' and 'off balance' activities whilst moving

▶ create a dance which starts on the spot and finishes by filling the whole room space with action. Name this dance 'A time to be born'. Think about animals, plants and insects as well as human births

▶ continue this exploration into the use of personal and general space with the 'Incredible Egg' *dance idea*

10 *The Egg Dances*

The Easter egg family

KEY STAGE 1
Accompaniment: Voice sounds, body percussion and the *Humpty Dumpty* nursery rhyme

Start individually, growing into bigger and bigger shapes then bursting out of sharp, jagged 'egg' shapes:

► use the *Humpty Dumpty* nursery rhyme with young ones to reinforce and accompany the 'egg' idea

► organise the class into small group 'nest' circles. The egg family consists of Mr, Mrs, Master and Miss 'Egg'. They grow into their own egg shapes; then hatch

► create follow-my-leader lines with the egg family waddling with bent elbows, changing leaders and jumping and clapping, changing again and wibbling and wobbling

► finish the dance of the egg family in one long class follow-my-leader line which tiptoes around the room until it has made a class 'nest' circle

► repeat the 'egg dance' as a class group, i.e.

> Growing into egg shapes
> Breaking out in spiky shapes
> A follow-my-leader line
> A finishing circle shape

The incredible egg

KEY STAGE 2

Accompaniment: *The Hall of the Mountain King* from *Peer Gynt* by Grieg

The egg hatches. Encourage a variety of strong, slow pushing actions contrasted with sudden, short, jabbing actions:

► a creature emerges: what is it? Use the imagination to show and exaggerate how the creature moves, the direction in which it travels, its size, weight and speed

► discuss where the creature lives and create an imaginary environment using props and apparatus if necessary

► a cave creature: work on exploring and searching the cave; follow-my-leader footsteps; tiptoeing around rockpools

► create a dance in threes entitled *The incredible egg*.

A creature emerges

11 Body Shapes

Playdough and pastry shapes

KEY STAGE 1
Accompaniment: The story of *The Gingerbread Man*

Playdough and a rolling pin are useful for experimental work on shapes. As you roll out the playdough the children flatten their shapes along the floor, then, as you twist the dough upwards, the shapes grow up too:

▶ explore the reactions of the children when you curl the dough into a ball, roll it along the ground, pull it in different directions and so on

▶ older children can develop the playdough idea into pair work with one child playing the sculptor and the other being 'sculpted' into a variety of shapes

► the story of *The Gingerbread Man* brings pastry shapes to life. It starts with you 'in role' as the little old lady rolling the pastry. The children roll in a ball along the floor. Then they stretch from curled, round shapes to long, thin ones, extending their arms, fingers, legs and toes. You pretend to place on each child two bright, beady, currant eyes, a cherry nose and an orange peel mouth. When you clap, the children jump up with legs and arms stretched wide and a mischievous expression. Keeping this shape they walk, run and finally dance happily around the movement space.

Objects, costumes and props

KEY STAGE 2
Accompaniment: Voice sounds

Props – a large piece of material

54

Make a collection of natural objects such as shells, stones, leaves and plants. Ask the children to grow and shrink into the different shapes either individually or in small groups:

▶ use photographs or observations of man-made objects such as buildings, windows, spiral staircases and chimneys, and in small groups or as individuals in one big class group, ask the children to create a 'man-made skyline' with their body shapes

▶ a large piece of material can form a cloak which can be whirled symmetrically round and round the body. Using knees, elbows, fingers and feet, the children can grow upwards into jagged, spiky shapes. Thus, one shape turns and whirls and the other jumps and hops. Ask the children to create group shapes using material, and to change shapes whilst moving

▶ elastic can be used to highlight stretching and curling into different shapes at different speeds. In pairs, it forms symmetric and asymmetric lines. Try weaving a huge spider's web in small groups or even in a large class group. The perfect spider's web is one of the most symmetric forms, but it can soon be broken and disorganised into asymmetry.

12 *Changing Shapes*

KEY STAGE 1

Accompaniment: A variety of nursery rhymes. The action rhyme:

'As tall as a house;
as small as a mouse;
as wide as a gate;
as thin as a pin!'

▶ Many nursery rhyme characters demonstrate shapes in action and changing shapes, e.g. *Humpty Dumpty* stretches and grows, rocks and rolls, tips and wobbles and finally falls off his wall and cracks into tiny, jagged pieces. Then there is the *crooked man* with his spiky fingers, crooked elbows and knocking, knobbly knees; the *crooked cat* creeping with paws and claws turned inwards; the *crooked mouse* with high bent knees and spiky elbows and constant changes of direction along crooked pathways. The *crooked house* emerges bit by bit into a whole class group shape.

Puppets – changing shape

▶ Nursery stories such as *The Ugly Duckling* and *Pinocchio*, the puppet boy, also demonstrate changing shapes.

▶ Play a 'statues' shape game where the children finish in one of the four basic body shapes – as wide as a wall, as tall as a tree, as round as a ball and as twisted as a screw. Then try to find 'tall' ways of walking; 'wide' ways of jumping, 'round' ways of rolling and 'twisted' ways of turning.

▶ Early explorations on shape rely on growing and shrinking. As confidence and skill develop, the children can be encouraged to experiment with moving from one shape to the next in increasingly adventurous ways – with a jump, a spin, a leap, a stretch, a fall, a roll. These transition actions are as important as the shapes themselves.

Accompaniment: *Tubular Bells* by Mike Oldfield

Improvise using a variety of ways of changing from one body shape to another, for example, by stretching, curling, twisting, jumping, rolling, stepping and so on:

▶ using the four basic body shapes, wall, ball, arrow and screw, make shapes which stay on the spot and transitions which travel into another space

▶ create new shapes at high, low or medium levels and change shapes either by travelling, jumping or turning

▶ take a trip through a hall of mirrors – the kind you see at a fairground. Explore the possibilities of this task to create numerous, humorous body shapes and to create a dance comedy

▶ improvise on a variety of transitions from shape to shape. Search for variety in shape – tall, wide, spiky, wobbly, short, balanced, grotesque

▶ use stepping, turning, jumping, running, rolling to create a variety of transitions between different shapes

▶ work on the interaction between shapes and pathways, for example, the 'arrow' shape can divide the 'wall' or pierce the rounded 'ball' shapes: the 'screw' twists and weaves its way in and out of the 'wall' and surrounds the 'ball' shape. Try working on each body shape as a group unit and then interacting with other groups.

13 *Shadows*

The Shadow

'On sunny days I am never free,
For I have a friend who comes with me.
He says no word, he makes no sound,
Yet I know well that he will be found
On the ground or up the wall,
Spread and flat or twelve feet tall.

I curl myself up like a ball:
He changes too, to very small.
I stretch right out, all long and thin,
And there he is, just like a pin.
I make myself feel like a screw,
But know, of course, he will do it too.

I rush along with huge great paces,
But he comes too – in fact, he races.
I test him out, and go so slow.
Confound the fellow! Why won't he go?
To catch him out, I jump up high.
At last I've got him. He can't fly.'

by Edith Stokes
from *Word Pictures* (Macdonald, out of print)

KEY STAGE 1
Accompaniment: Selected phrases from *The Shadow* by Edith Stokes

Start with minor images. First, with the class copying your hand gestures and then growing and shrinking into mirror images of your shapes. You might choose one child instead of yourself to lead this activity:

▶ repeat this mirroring activity in pairs

▶ take the children outdoors on a sunny day to observe their own shadow shapes as well as those of buildings, trees, and other objects. Explore some of the ideas in the rhyme and let the children make shadowy shapes of their own

▶ play follow-my-leader shadows in pairs. The child in front leads her partner with slow, controlled steps, stopping from time to time to make still, balanced shapes at high and low levels, which the other child must copy

▶ stress the part of the poem where the child tries to lose the shadow. Play simple games using slow and fast travelling and jumping actions whilst trying to escape from the shadow

▶ let the children suggest and practise ways of trying to lose their shadows by sudden jumps, upwards, sideways or backwards; by zig-zag running or by using turning, falling, rolling and tiptoeing actions.

KEY STAGE 2
Accompaniment: *The Shadow* by Edith Stokes

Start with the group facing the leader and mirroring a variety of body shapes – high, low, wide and twisted:

▶ repeat in pairs first mirroring each other and then in follow-my-leader formation

▶ use the poem as the stimulus for a 'shadow dance' in pairs with the emphasis on the transitions between the shadow shapes – using stepping, turning, jumping, running etc

▶ try a variety of relationship possibilities, for example, facing each other, side by side, one behind the other

▶ close eyes and/or turn out the lights and think about the shadows and shapes of the night. Introduce creatures of the night and create a dance based on night-time shadows

▶ use one line, one verse or the whole poem as the stimulus and/or accompaniment for a duet called 'The Shadow'.

The shadow – a duet

Symmetry and Asymmetry

KEY STAGE 1

Accompaniment: The action rhymes, *Simon Says* and *As Tall as a House*

▶ Play a game of *Simon Says* with the class spaced out facing you and give them various movement commands prefaced by the words 'Simon says'. Ask the children to obey the commands only when they are prefaced with these words and when the movement is symmetrical –

'Simon says jump up tall'
'Simon says shrink down small'
'Simon says stretch out wide'.

Try to catch the children out by interspersing symmetrical movements with asymmetrical ones, for example, 'hop on one foot' and 'reach high and low'. Older children can lead this game themselves.

▶ Face the class group, or organise the children in pairs. Ask them to mirror the four basic body shapes – round and curled (a ball), stretched and wide (a wall), twisting and turning (a screw), thin and pointed (an arrow). Move from one shape to the next, pointing out that the ball shape is symmetrical, the screw shape is asymmetrical and that the arrow and wall shapes can be either symmetrical or asymmetrical.

▶ Encourage the children to find their very own symmetric and asymmetric body shapes. A collection of interesting things of different shapes and sizes will extend and develop the children's ideas of what shapes they can make. Such objects can range from things found in the natural world (animals, plants, shells, logs, stones) to man-made goods (wheels, toys, dolls, robots, teddy bears). This is an excellent way for young children to bring symmetry to life and to make shapes move.

KEY STAGE 2
Accompaniment: *Variations* by Andrew Lloyd Webber

▶ Arrange the children in pairs facing each other and mirroring each others' actions. Ask them to twist and stretch their bodies into all sorts of extraordinary shapes. Allow creative freedom, but encourage clarity by making sure that each shape is held for a few seconds before the next shape is assumed, so that the symmetric and asymmetric nature of the shape can be established.

▶ Explore moving from shape to shape in a variety of different orders, for example, from ball to arrow to screw to wall, or from wall to ball to arrow to screw and develop this activity by asking the children to make each shape move to another space in a symmetric or an asymmetric way. So, the ball shape can roll in different directions. The wall shape can sway, step or jump sideways; the screw shape can turn slowly and quickly, and move up and down; the arrow shape can advance forwards and retreat backwards, stepping, running and piercing through space:

Symmetric body shapes

▶ create new body shapes and experiment with symmetrical and asymmetrical shapes at high and low levels, on the spot and in travelling

▶ in groups of fours, fives, sixes and sevens, experiment with creating group shapes that are symmetrical

▶ explore the following statements:
asymmetric shapes often cause imbalance and so the body tips over and begins to travel
symmetric shapes are virtually static
it is possible for the balanced shapes of symmetry to move and the imbalanced shapes of asymmetry to remain still.

14 Shape Pictures

Shapes

'Fine crystal shapes arrived in the night;
Frosted fern pictures, gleaming bright white
On the window-pane. Who put them there?
Artistry created with such care,
What we know will not last a day
And a glimpse of sun will melt away.

Man-made chimneys, solid, powerful,
Awesome, dominating, purposeful,
Smoke, which, depending on the weather,
May cover all like a vast umbrella,
Or lazily drift, or belch up high –
By day stark white, at night tints the sky.

Old gnarled oak – firm, twisted and strong,
Sensitive willow that weeps all day long,
Flat disc-like sun, the crescent moon,
Rings in the pond from a pebble thrown;
And long rays of light at early dawn
Show spiders' webs, precise in their form.'

By Edith Stokes
from *Word Pictures* (Macdonald, out of print)

Use this poem to stimulate creative dance 'pictures' based on contrasting shapes and patterns.

KEY STAGE 1

Accompaniment: Images and phrases from *'Shapes'* by Edith Stokes

Extract only those images which can be understood at this stage, for example, ice patterns on the window-pane, chimneys blowing out thick smoke, the gnarled oak tree, the weeping willow, the round sun, the crescent moon, a spider's web:

▶ use the above images to make shapes individually, in small and in class groups. Bring visual material to the lesson to reinforce the images if possible

► create dances based on Jack Frost – a spiky, icy little man, painting the trees and houses frosty white; a forest – full of twisted, stretched, spiky, drooping and tangled trees, branches and undergrowth; a spider's web – made by stretching out arms and legs and reaching at high and low levels.

KEY STAGE 2

Accompaniment: A recorded version of the poem *'Shapes'* by Edith Stokes

Record a spoken version of the poem:

► improvise around the shape images in the poem

► create a short solo using the recorded poem

► choose two contrasting images and make dance phrases which describe these through actions

► work in pairs, then in groups of four to six to create a dance based on the shape images within the poem, but do not use the recorded poem or have it spoken out loud.

 *Spatial Explorations*

An imaginary journey

KEY STAGE 1

Accompaniment: *Fun Fair* from *Holiday Diary* by Benjamin Britten

All sorts of new spatial concepts can be introduced during an imaginary journey:

► use the following words to enhance the possibilities: over/under; around/through; towards/away from

► introduce the idea of 'props', for example, hoops to move through, benches to balance on, gymnastic apparatus to clamber over, under, around and between

► take the apparatus away and lead the class through a journey: start with moving along straight and curved pathways

► introduce changes in speed and level

► act as explorers moving over, under, around and through a dense forest

- divide the class in half then ask them to form groups of three: one half grows into tangled undergrowth shapes and the other half creeps under, over, around and through. Change over so that everyone has a chance to practise

- extend the imaginary journey so that the explorers move through forests and jungles, over mountains, beneath oceans and on distant planets.

KEY STAGE 2

Accompaniment: *Incantations* by Incantations, South American traditional musicians

Move in different ways along constrasting pathways at high, low and medium levels:

- use hoops, ropes, elastic, chalked pathways and long, flowing pieces of material to create an environment to move towards, along, away from, around, through, beneath and above

- create phrases of movement containing jumps, falls, rolls, stretches, twists and bends

An imaginary journey

- experiment with balance and off balance
- improvise using different relationship possibilities, for example, action and reaction, leader and follower, moving simultaneously, moving in turn
- make dances in pairs, threes or fours, with or without props, based on the idea of an obstacle race

  All the suggestions within this idea can be transferred to other imaginary situations such as: a haunted house; a jungle journey; man in space; brave explorers.

 ## 16 *Spirals*

Accompaniment: Overture from *Midsummer Night's Dream* by Mendelssohn

Bring a series of spiralling shapes and objects to the lesson, for example, a bedspring, a shell, a screw, a paper spiral:

- start with individual interpretations using hands only
- try spiralling from high, wide shapes to low, curled shapes and vice versa
- change the speed so that the children spiral suddenly, then slowly
- change the strength so that sometimes the spiral twists, turns and screws itself downwards slowly and heavily, and sometimes whirls and curls lightly
- progress to spiralling floor patterns which are formed by making a class follow-my-leader line and travelling round and round in ever decreasing circles towards the middle of the room
- unwind a spiralling floor pattern by facing the opposite way so that the person at the back of the line becomes the new leader
- introduce the idea of a giant-sized snake spiralling and coiling inwards, then spiralling and unravelling outwards.

KEY STAGE 2
Accompaniment: *The Snow is Dancing* from *A Children's Corner* by Debussy

Start with spiralling arm gestures, with eyes following the movement of the hands:

▶ make a spiral on the spot which shrinks as it sinks and extends as it rises or opens as the body sinks and closes as the body rises

▶ spiral from high to low to high whilst travelling and turning to a new space

▶ explore spiralling with a partner moving in unison; at different levels; with contrasting speeds and strengths; on the spot and to another space

▶ add spiralling floor pattern, in leader/follower pairs, or group lines, or individually

▶ create a dance in pairs, then in fours, which explores spiralling air and floor patterns.

Spiralling with a partner

Patterns and Pathways

Patterns in the air, patterns on the floor

KEY STAGE 1

Accompaniment: *Ase's Death* from the *Peer Gynt Suite* by Grieg

Use one finger to draw two contrasting patterns in the air – long, straight lines/short, zig-zag lines; straight lines/round circles; wavy lines/ smooth circles; zig-zag/wavy lines:

▶ make the patterns above into pathways on the floor

▶ contrast the speed of each pattern

▶ create changes in level

▶ work with a partner using one pattern only to form a meeting and parting dance and encourage the children to move one at a time, as well as both at the same time.

Lines, patterns and pathways

KEY STAGE 2

Accompaniment: *Lines* by Deborah Bestwick

Use this extract from the poem to form a dance based on lines, patterns and pathways:

'Straight lines, long lines,
Curved lines, short lines,
Thick lines, thin lines
Horizontal, vertical,
Parallel and spiral
Diagonal and zig-zag.
All sorts of lines . . .'

▶ link floor and air patterns to form phrases of curved, flexible, fluid movements contrasted with straight, linear actions

▶ try moving in different ways along contrasting pathways, for example: stamp along straight lines with a sudden turn to face a new direction where a wall or a barrier is confronted

▶ run along curved, twisting lines weaving in and out of spaces
hop along zig-zags changing feet on each change of direction
tiptoe around circles and spirals

Hop along zig-zag lines

Each line of the extract from the poem has contrasting pathways written into it. Work line by line, with a partner, through the poem. In your partner dance make sure that you:

▶ work alone sometimes;

▶ move on the spot as well as through the room space;

▶ show contrasts in the air as well as floor patterns;

▶ use contrasting relationships such as meeting and parting, leader and follower.

18 Circles

Accompaniment: Action rhyme: *The wheels on the bus go round and round*; *Fun Fair* from *Holiday Diary* by Benjamin Britten; *The Ball* from *Children's Games* by Bizet

▶ Organise the children into circles by spreading outwards. Start in the centre of the room with the children seated around you, then rise up slowly on tiptoes and stretch and spread outwards together.

▶ Try a follow-my-leader – start with the children spaced out, then tiptoe amongst them, gently touching one by one until all are following in a long class line. Lead the line around the outside of the room until a circle is formed.

Fairground circles

Create a fairground full of roundabouts, big wheels and small wheels all turning and spinning:

▶ the class circle is an ideal formation for the big wheel. Start with the children stretching from low curled shapes to form wide wheel spokes. Ask them to reach towards the fingers or toes of the person next to them. Use a hand bell to indicate when the children should change their stretched shapes from high to low and vice versa. Soon, very slowly, the circle will be able to turn round and round as the children reach up high and down low.

▶ an everyday theme which is rich in circle shapes and games is water: use one finger, then one toe (the children will need to pivot on one foot) to draw a 'circular puddle' around them. Try tiptoeing around the puddle and jumping into the centre to make an imaginary splash, then jump back out again.

▶ puddle shapes can be made in small and large groups or by placing hoops on the floor to tiptoe around and to jump in and out of: try not to be caught in the puddle when the music stops.

KEY STAGE 2
Accompaniment: *Bolero* by Ravel

In small groups work on what can be done with a circle. The circle can revolve clockwise and anti-clockwise. It can expand and contract. It can rise and fall. It can be symmetric or asymmetric with actions happening in unison or one after the other. The dancers may face inwards or outwards or both. The possibilities are many and varied:

▶ create large, circular patterns in the air with arms and with legs

▶ make the circles even bigger by asking them to advance forwards and retreat backwards (like a wheel); open, turn and close (like a round table); reach to one side then circle over to the other side and back to the start (like a huge round hole in a wall)

▶ put two groups together, one inside the other, and explore the possibilities of circles moving within circles

▶ explore the cyclic nature of the circle bringing in the life cycles of animals, insects and humans

▶ create a dance based on the statement: 'A line has a clear beginning and a definite ending, but a circle goes on and on and on until it is broken.'

Dynamic Dance

Dynamic dance

The dynamic qualities of dance add colour and rhythm to the action. The emphasis is on how the body moves: quickly, slowly, powerfully, gently, directly, sharply, floppily, alertly, lazily . . .

There are two major learning areas:

Dynamic contrasts – which deal with changes in the
weight (light and strong)
time (quick and slow)
flow (continuous and interrupted)
direction (direct and indirect)

Rhythm – including explorations into metric and non-metric possibilities, body rhythms and the use of sounds, words, live and recorded music.

The National Curriculum is equally emphatic, but less specific, about the dynamic qualities of dance.

At Key Stage 1 it states that the children should:

▶ be helped to develop rhythmic responses

▶ experience working with a range and variety of contrasting stimuli, particularly music

▶ be given opportunities to explore moods and feelings through spontaneous responses and through structured tasks

▶ explore contrasts of speed, tension, continuity, and describe what they have done.

Expressing feelings and moods

Key Stage 2 goes further by asking for:

▶ complexity in body actions and step patterns (natural and imposed rhythmic structures)

▶ variation in the speed, tension and continuity of action

▶ responses to a range of stimuli to express feelings and moods.

19 Time Changes

Words can be used to create continuity or interrupt the flow of movement. They also have other inherent dynamic qualities. There are:

slow words – creep, crawl, slither, linger, glide, float, melt.
quick words – dart, dab, sparkle, flicker, flutter, shiver, startle.

KEY STAGE 1
Accompaniment: Slow and quick words

Ask the children to respond to each word spontaneously in an appropriate way. Encourage them to perform every action in a number of different ways:

▶ colour their imaginations by asking them to 'creep quietly like a cat'; 'glide like a bird'; 'dart like a mouse this way and that'; 'flicker like flames in a fire'

▶ find new ways to move slowly and quickly 'like a . . .' emphasise the changes in time.

▶ select words from those listed above to describe the way different animals and insects move, for example:

        cats – creep, dart, twist, dab
        birds – glide, float, flutter
        snakes – slither, linger, flicker
        bees – dart, dab, flutter, linger
        butterflies – glide, float, flutter, flicker

KEY STAGE 2
Accompaniment: Slow and quick words

Select words from those listed above to describe the different ways in which people, creatures and objects move.

▶ Improvise around two contrasting words to form short movement
'motifs' based on time changes, for example:
glide and flicker
flutter and slither
sparkle and melt
creep and dart.

▶ Improvise on at least two words and a maximum of five, to form action
phrases based on time changes. Introduce new words whenever
possible, for example:
curl – slither – startle – fade
bounce – roll – flick – slowly melt away
darting – darting – slowly sinking – leap and twirl away
silently – slowly – stealthily shrinking – BANG!
flashing – sparkling – flitting – darting – vanish
sparkle – spatter – shoot and swirl.

▶ create a dance in pairs based on:
things which go slowly
things which move fast.

Things which go slowly and things which go fast

74

Changes in Weight

The following words describe contrasting strong and light movements:
'Strong words' – pull, push, stamp, twist, whip, pound, bounce, loud.
'Light words' – glide, float, whirl, hover, flit, swirl, soft, bounce. Some
words, for example, 'bounce' can be performed strongly or lightly.

KEY STAGE 1
Accompaniment: Strong and light words. Percussive sounds

Use your voice and a tambourine to create a series of loud and soft
sounds. Ask the children to respond spontaneously in movement:

▶ choose one strong and one light word and ask the children to respond
spontaneously: repeat until all the words listed above have been
explored

▶ create 'loud and soft' dances using stamping, tiptoeing, clapping and
gesturing actions

▶ listen and react to pieces of music which contain loud and soft
phrases: nursery rhymes can be used for this purpose

▶ find new ways to move strongly and lightly: stamp like an elephant,
float with the clouds, pound like a hammer drill, whirl with the wind

▶ select words from those listed above to describe the way different
things move, for example:
ropes – pull, push, whip, twist
feathers – float, swivel, whirl, swirl
flies – flit, hover, whirl
waves – whirl, swirl, crash and pound.

Bring objects and pictures to the lesson to colour the children's imaginations.

KEY STAGE 2
Accompaniment: Strong and light words. Percussive sounds.
Twenty-Four Pieces for Children by Kabalevsky

Use percussive instruments to create contrasting phrases made up of
soft and loud sounds. Ask the children to react spontaneously and then to
structure their improvisations to form repeatable dance phrases:

▶ improvise around two contrasting words to form short movement
'motifs' based on weight changes, for example:

push and swirl
float and bounce
whirl and pound
glide and stamp

▶ improvise on at least two and a maximum of six words to form action phrases based on weight changes, introducing new words whenever possible, for example:
push – pull, stretch, curl, roll right away
stamp – tiptoe, clap, crash
flit – hover, swirl, curl
bounce – pound, whip, swirl
trickle – roll, crash, bounce, pound, swirl

▶ listen to recorded music and select excerpts from one or two pieces which depict strong and light/loud and soft actions: work in pairs to create a dance using the music as the stimulus for and maybe the accompaniment to your dance.

21 Dynamic Contrasts

Weight and time

KEY STAGE 1
Accompaniment: Hand-held percussion, action words

▶ Use a tambourine to play strong, sudden then strong and slow travelling phrases.

▶ Play light, sudden then light and slow phrases and ask the children to respond in their own ways.

▶ Move like animals which are:
strong/sudden – lion, panther, fox
light/sudden – cat, mouse, bird
strong/sustained – elephant, tortoise, snake
light/sustained – bird, butterfly, giraffe
(Some of these animals move with contrasting dynamics and can therefore stimulate varied dynamic dances.)

▶ Use the following words to illuminate dynamic contrasts:
explode like a volcano

whip round and round
dart like a fish
flicker like fire
press, pull and push
wring out the washing
glide through the air
float like a bubble.

▶ Dance with simple hand-held percussive instruments to create a short dance based on contrasts in weight (strong/light) and time (sudden/ sustained).

Contrasts in weight and time

Weight/time combinations

Accompaniment: Hand-held percussion. Cartoon Capers – music for cartoons

▶ Contrast moving strongly and suddenly with moving strongly and slowly, playing percussive phrases which the children react to.

▶ Use the improvisations above to create action and reaction phrases in pairs with one person moving slowly and the other moving suddenly. Change over so that both have the opportunity to move strongly in sudden and sustained ways.

▶ Investigate other contrasting movement phrases, for example, light, sudden actions followed by light, sustained recoveries – and in reverse; light, sustained actions followed by light, sudden recoveries.

Strong, sustained actions

▶ Explore the contrasts between weight and time through the following dynamic words:
strong/sudden – explode, punch, whip
light/sudden – dart, dash, flicker
strong/sustained – press, wring and pull
light/sustained – glide, float and smooth.

▶ Create dances based on cartoon characters such as *Tom and Jerry*, *Popeye* and *Micky Mouse*. Use the cartoon idea to demonstrate contrasts in weight (strong/light) and time (sudden/sustained).

KEY STAGE 1

Rhythmic rhymes

Accompaniment: Traditional action and nursery rhymes

Start with well-known rhymes such as *The Grand Old Duke of York*, marching and *Wee Willie Winkie*, running – and then introduce:

▶ more specific rhymes with clear rhythmic qualities

▶ stamping and clapping rhymes

> *Rain, rain, go away.*
> *Come again another day.*
> *Rain, rain, go away,*
> *Come again on washing day.*

> *We all clap hands together,*
> *We all clap hands together,*
> *We all clap hands together,*
> *As children like to do.*

▶ dancing rhymes – introduce recordings of favourite rhymes and songs for the children to dance to freely and ask them to bring in their own favourites to clap and dance to such as: *Hey diddle diddle, the cat and the fiddle* and:

> *Dance to your daddy, my little laddie*
> *Dance to your daddy, my little man*
> *You shall have a fishy on a little dishy*
> *You shall have a fishy when the boat comes in.*

▶ sing and chant and clap rhymes and rhythms frequently and create new rhymes of your own.

Repetitive rhythms

Accompaniment: Rhythmic rhymes

The following rhymes provide a variety of opportunities for clapping, stepping, skipping, marching, galloping, hopping and running. At this Key Stage it is the rhythm of the rhyme, not the words which are important, so omit the words when you are sure that the children have fully grasped the rhythm and tempo.

A going and stopping rhyme:

Higgledy, piggledy pop!
The dog has eaten the mop.
The pie's in a hurry,
The cat's in a flurry,
Higgledy, piggledy pop!

A hopping and jumping rhyme:

One potato, two potato, three potato, four,
Five potato, six potato, seven potato more.

The hornpipe rhythm makes this rhyme suitable for hopping, galloping, pulling and pushing:

A sailor went to sea, sea, sea
To see what he could see, see, see
And all that he could see, see, see
Was the bottom of the deep blue sea, sea, sea.

▶ Make a rhythmic pattern based on the rhythms of first names. For example, Susannah has three syllables so the rhythmic pattern might be a hop, a step and a jump. Sam, in contrast, can choose only to move with a jump or a stamp once, or to repeat his name to create a rhythmic pattern – Sam, Sam . . . Sam, Sam, Sam . . . hop, jump . . . run, run, run.

▶ Older children will enjoy moving slowly across the rhythmic pattern as well as performing the pattern literally.

▶ Create short dance sequences based on hopscotch, playground chants and skipping-rope games.

23 Natural Body Rhythms

The human body has its own in-built rhythms and does not always need stimulus from an external sound. Music is not an indispensable part of creative movement and dance work. Children will happily and productively explore and create rhythmic body actions without any accompaniment.

KEY STAGE 1
No Accompaniment

The ideas that follow will help the children to structure and vary the dynamic qualities of whole body actions – jumping, turning, travelling, growing and shrinking.

▶ *Jumping* – make regular, rhythmic bouncing jumps; long stretched leaps and sudden explosive jumps. Hop and jump in different body shapes. Run and stretch out wide, roll and close and curl. Balance, with one part of the body opened and one part closed. Open out one part of the body, suddenly or slowly, while the rest stays still. Jumping actions of animals, insects and birds vary the quality of movement.

▶ *Turning* – punctuate sudden spinning turns with statue stops and slow, spiralling turns with changes of level. Encourage the children to observe and interpret the rhythmic movement of things that turn – wheels, clocks, balls, leaves, roundabouts, turntables.

▶ *Travelling* – contrast giant strides and tiny tiptoe steps; creeping and stamping; trotting and galloping; skipping and marching; crawling and slithering. Listen to the rhythms of different footsteps and interpret them through a variety of travelling actions.

▶ *Growing and Shrinking* – grow quickly and shrink slowly, then grow slowly and shrink quickly. Stretch and turn; jump and shrink.

KEY STAGE 2
No Accompaniment

▶ Experiment with changes in speed, strength, duration and flow so that, for example, the difference is felt between a series of short, spinning terms and one long, lingering opening and turning action and/or short, bouncing jumps and long, extended leaps.

▶ Combine the turning and jumping actions above to form rhythmic phrases. Choose other contrasts such as long and short gestures combined with loud and soft feet.

▶ Explore through improvisation the following three dance qualities:
> slow, gentle, day dreaming
> quick, lively, excited
> strong, forceful, bossy.

Establish a short dance for each character.

▶ In threes, choose one character each. Then create a dance, a conversation without any words or accompaniment. Use the following to help structure the dance:
> moving one at a time
> leader and follower relationships
> question and answer relationships
> advancing and retreating
> moving in harmony
> moving in conflict.

The moods may be interchangeable.

Percussion Instruments

Hand-held percussion instruments can be used both to control the action taking place and to elicit varied rhythmic responses from the children.

Percussion instruments suitable for use with Key Stage 1 and 2 pupils fall into three categories:

▶ rhythmic, beating sounds – drums, rhythm sticks, wood blocks, hollow skull shapes

▶ melodic, ringing sounds – cymbals and finger cymbals, triangles, chime bars

▶ rattling, shaking sounds – tambourines, bells, maracas, castanets.

KEY STAGE 1
Accompaniment: Hand-held percussion

▶ Demonstrate the potential of each instrument yourself by asking the children to respond spontaneously to the sounds you produce. A drum can imitate a dripping tap or a band of marching soldiers. It can beat out a simple repetitive rhythm or, scratched with fingernails, it can accompany slow curling and stretching.

▶ When each child has an instrument issue three basic rules:

start moving and playing only to a given signal

when each of you has finished, stand still and quiet until all the others have finished too

all instruments must be placed on the floor when you all sit down to listen.

▶ Help the children to appreciate that there is an enormous difference between purposeful dancing and playing and aimless hitting and moving. Set short, easily achievable tasks such as *run with the bells shaking*, or *stamp to the sound of the drum* to test out and reinforce these rules.

▶ The children will soon be able to select suitable instruments for specific themes. Try out as dance stimulus ideas:
> a firework display
> a dripping tap
> weather
> toys and machines.

▶ Older children will be able to dance in pairs and small groups with their instruments.

KEY STAGE 2
Accompaniment: Hand-held percussion

▶ Observe the three rules set out in Key Stage 1 and start with the teacher playing and the children responding.

▶ Give each child the same category of instrument, for example, rhythmic, beating, melodic, ringing or rattling and shaking.

If you do not have access to enough of these, try making your own instruments out of yoghurt pots, plastic bottles, milk bottle tops, tins and large tin lids. Dried beans and lentils in a box or tin make good shaking noises.

Experiment with all sorts of different ways to move with the instrument and use demonstrations from the class group to improve the quality and contrasts within the action.

▶ Devise short percussion sequences with a leader and a follower, holding a movement conversation in which the first child plays and moves to one sound and the second replies with a contrasting sound and movement.

▶ It is not necessary for all the children to dance and play throughout the movement session; a small group can play percussion instruments while the others move. Change the groups frequently so that everyone has a chance to dance and to play.

A movement conversation

▶ Begin with short, simple phrases, either worked out in advance or developed with the movement. A good starting point is familiar nursery rhymes or popular classics with a regular beat, such as, *Boys and Girls Come Out to Play* or *The March of the Toreadors* by Bizet. The musicians shake and tap the rhythms while the dancers skip, turn and jump.

Try these:

▶ the musicians play the rhythms of individual children's names while the others stamp and clap

▶ the musicians play their own sound patterns for the dancers to interpret in movement and the dancers make their own movement patterns for the musicians to interpret in sound.

25 Musical Opposites

KEY STAGE 1

Accompaniment: *Listen to the Music Play* – a rhyme

'Listen to the music play –
What's the music got to say?
Does it go? . . . and,
Does it stop?
Does it turn around a lot?

Can you hear the marching beat?

Can you hear the marching beat?
Or the sound of tiptoe feet.
Listen to the music play –
It's time to move in your own way!'

► Use the rhyme above to highlight moving in opposite kinds of ways, for example, travelling with running, tiptoeing, hopping, skipping and jumping steps; turning quickly and slowly, up high and down low.

► Create new action phrases based on the phrase: *Slow, slow, quick, quick, slow*. Stress listening before moving and suggest alternate phrases of quick, quiet running and long, slow stepping.

► Play contrasting pieces of music to accompany the poem and to provide a *listen, then move* exercise.

► In pairs create an *opposite* dance moving quickly and slowly; strongly and lightly. Emphasise moving one at a time and use voice, percussion or music to indicate the speed and strength.

KEY STAGE 2

Accompaniment: Selected musical excerpts, for example *Carnival of the Animals* by Saint-Saens

► Select a series of contrasting musical phrases from a popular classical recording and use these phrases to create dances in pairs. Record several *musical opposites* which highlight changes in pitch (high and low), volume (loud and soft), duration (long and short), weight (strong and light) and time (quick and slow).

Musical moods

▶ Use the idea of musical moods to stimulate a dance for a small group (four to six) people with each person creating a dance around the following moods:

happy talk – a lively skipping and jumping dance

sad songs – sinking, growing, curling, rolling or slowly stepping

an angry dance – making strong shapes, using clapping, stamping and percussive body sounds

shy talk – moving away from, then back towards the group – finishing alone

▶ Create musical opposites using hand-held percussion and making musical phrases whilst moving. Feet can be used as the stimulus and accompaniment to a variety of musical opposites:

big feet – with enormous plodding steps

small feet – with tiny, baby feet toddling and tiptoeing

fast feet – moving quickly and lightly, with sudden statue stops

slow feet – emphasise the exaggerated 'slow motion' qualities

▶ Try this in leader/follower formation; as an action sequence; as an echo dance; or as a movement conversation.

▶ Create a dramatic dance based on conflict and confrontation by thinking (in movement terms) of opposites such as rival groups of people; day and night; fire and water; colour clashing.

 **26** *Follow the Band*

KEY STAGE 1
Accompaniment: Suitable recorded 'band' music

▶ *Follow-my-leader* – play contrasting rhythms for the group to respond to – marching then skipping.

▶ *The brass band* – choose military style brass band music. Start by listening, then clap and stamp to its regular repetitive rhythms. Add marching in and out of spaces with sudden stops, salutes and changes in direction. Add 'drummers drumming' and 'bugles blowing' as the lines march in single and double file.

▶ *A steel band* – get the children shimmering and shaking accompanied by live or recorded steel band music. Try dancing with shakers, bells and tambourines to add to the 'carnival' atmosphere of the steel band.

▶ Try out other types of band music, for example, a country dance band, a folk and a pop group.

▶ Put the dances which follow the band into the context of a *carnival parade*.

Follow the band

KEY STAGE 2

Accompaniment: Pre-recorded musical extracts of band music from different parts of the world

▶ Provide extracts of music on tape with contrasting rhythms and styles. Listen and talk about each one in turn and then work on interpreting each one differently in movement.

▶ Develop the idea of following the band by introducing music from different parts of the world:
Africa – step patterns and drumming
India – hand, arm and foot gestures
Spain and South America – rhythmic foot and finger tapping
Greece – turning, stepping, clapping.

Hand, arm and foot gestures

▶ Work on traditional country dance forms from the United Kingdom and from the rest of Europe.

▶ Introduce a caricature of a *pop group* with 'exaggerated' musicians wearing cartoon type masks, and playing drums, guitars, keyboards and vocals. Create short dance phrases around each instrument, for example:
the guitar player rises, sinks and turns
the drummer hops and jumps from foot to foot, side to side
the trombone player rises, sinks and steps forwards and backwards
the keyboard player and vocalist move towards and away from each other.

Maintain control by pressing the pause button to create stopping points.

Be wary and selective about using the children's own musical choices!

Echo Dances

KEY STAGE 1

Accompaniment: Voice sounds/BBC 'sound effects' records and tapes

Record your own echoes, or use the BBC Sound Effects Library. Play these echoes to the children to reinforce their understanding of sound echoes.

▶ Ask the children to echo simple percussive sounds with appropriate actions so that their movement echoes the music.

▶ Play short recorded pieces of music. Ask the children to echo the speed and strength of the music with their actions.

▶ Act as leader and perform very simple action phrases, for example, stamp, stamp, stamp . . . hop, jump, hop . . . creep, run, freeze . . . stretch slowly, shrink suddenly. Ask the children to echo your actions. Make sure that you move one after the other, *not* both at the same time!

▶ Adapt *Simon Says* to form an echoing game, i.e. the follower must repeat and echo the leader's actions only when *Simon Says*.

▶ Create a dance in pairs which explores echoing single actions and short movement sequences. Make sure the dance is on the spot – then travelling into spaces.

KEY STAGE 2

Accompaniment: Selected, pre-recorded, musical extracts, for example, Mussorsky: *Pictures at an Exhibition*

▶ Provide extracts of music with contrasting rhythms and styles. Listen and talk about each one in turn and then work on interpreting them in movement.

▶ Echo, with appropriate actions, the sounds of percussion or voice. Move after the sound, not with it.

▶ Echo the actions of a group leader. Again, move one after the other and keep the movement simple.

▶ Echo a given step pattern, for example, *slow, slow, quick, quick, slow*. Repeat this exercise in pairs. Create an echo dance with a partner where one dancer leads and the other echoes. Use recorded music at first, but then ask each pair to echo their actions unaccompanied. Emphasise the exact reproduction of timing, strength and body action.

▶ Introduce jumping strongly, then jumping lightly in turn.

▶ Add turning slowly and quickly.

▶ Create short travelling phrases, sometimes quick, sometimes slow and vary the strength of action.

▶ Give each pair two of the same percussion instruments which will stimulate and accompany the action.

▶ Let each partner have the opportunity to lead and to echo the actions.

Echoing the action

Time

Clocks

KEY STAGE 1
Accompaniment: A ticking clock; a metronome; The clock rhyme

Imitate the clock's regular ticking with actions of the hands, arms, legs and feet in circular clockwise motion.

► Use this rhyme as the stimulus and accompaniment to repetitive rhythmic actions:

'The clock ticks,
The clock tocks,
This way,
That way
And never, never stops.
Tick, tock . . .
Tick, tock.'

► Move forwards and backwards and from side to side like a metronome.

► Introduce robots and clockwork toys to help the children with these actions and with moving in regular stepping patterns.

► Play the game *Oranges and Lemons* with the emphasis on moving like the different clock bells – the big 'ding-dong' bell of Ben, the ringing bells of St Martin's, the booming bells of Old Bailey and the melodic bells of St Clement's.

► Listen to other rhythmic bell sounds and move with them – church bells, bus bells, bicycle bells, shop bells, school bells, handbells and door bells.

Machines

KEY STAGE 2
Accompaniment: Voice sounds, recorded machine sounds

One of the easiest ways of demonstrating how man has made use of machines is to develop a movement piece based on road-working machines.

► Develop movement ideas individually for road workers using picks, shovels, drills and hammers. Show hammer drills pounding; pneumatic drills shaking then stopping; mechanical diggers stretching and scooping; steam rollers rolling and turning.

► Working in threes or fours, children can make up an imaginary machine, with each child playing a different part of the whole and moving in different ways. For example, a clock with its controlled tick, tock, tick, tock; a typewriter with a tap, tap, tap . . . tap, tap, tap . . . tap . . . ping; a washing machine with its slosh, gurgle, slosh.

► Read poems about machines that develop a rhythm pattern.

Road workers

▶ Let the children create their own voice sounds and actions for a piece based, for example on a train journey. They develop different sounds and movements as the train goes through different situations – starting, gathering speed, going through cuttings, open country or tunnels, going under and over bridges, across level crossings, slowing down and stopping.

▶ Explore the movements of turning wheels, jumping pistons and levers pushing and pulling. Ask what the machine does and how each part works, in order to clarify the shape and quality of the actions.

▶ Make a class machine. Stand the children in a circle. Each child is a machine part: switch on all the different parts by touching the head of each child in turn. Then try putting the machine into low gear by asking the class to perform their machine actions in slow motion. Contrast the controlled, slow motion actions when the machine is in low gear with the sudden, jerky actions of a machine in top gear.

▶ Develop the idea of moving parts in machines making sounds, which in turn form rhythmic patterns.

Dance form

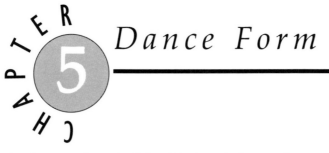

Dance Form

At the very heart of the National Curriculum recommendations for dance, is the ***art of making dances***. From the earliest age school pupils are encouraged to 'experience, and be guided towards, making dances with clear beginnings, middles and ends'.

In the End of Key Statements for Dance and PE, pupils at Key Stage 1 should be able to show that they can:

▶ plan and perform safely a range of simple actions and linked movements in response to given tasks and stimuli

▶ practise and improve their performance

▶ describe what they and others are doing.

(Key Stage 1: End of Key Stage Statement)

In the programmes of study specific to dance at Key Stage 2 pupils should:

▶ make dances with clear beginnings, middles and ends involving improvising, exploring, selecting and refining content, and sometimes incorporating work from other aspects of the curriculum, in particular music, art and drama.

Thus by seven years of age, pupils are being asked to compose, perform and appreciate their own dances and those of others. At the age of eleven this composition process should be well established in that pupils are expected to:

▶ plan, practise, improve and remember more complex sequences of movement

▶ evaluate how well they and others perform and behave against criteria suggested by the teacher and suggest ways of improving performance.

(Key Stage 2: End of Key Stage Statement)

This chapter, through a wide range of contrasting cross-curriculum dance ideas, uses several commonly accepted choreographic devices to help teachers and pupils to create and organise their own dances.

It starts with the formation of simple sequences or dance motifs and includes dances which move into maths; make believe; through the seasons; day by day; into the past and into the future.

The culmination is a complete dance performance of *The Wizard of Oz*: the dance-making process of composition, performance and appreciation can be experienced by all in a 'theatrical' context.

29 Dance Motifs

Motifs are the result of improvisation

A dance motif is a short pattern of movement which expresses and communicates a mood, a feeling, an activity or an idea.

Motifs are the result of improvisation. They come about through trial and error and eventually can be performed, repeated and built upon.

When creating a motif explore these possibilities:

▶ body activities: body parts in use

▶ dynamics, rhythm and tempo

▶ spatial placement: level, direction, pattern

▶ relationships: numbers dancing, formations.

Motif action

KEY STAGE 1
Accompaniment: Action words

▶ Practise simple combinations of movement:

> run and stop
> jump and turn
> rise and spread
> sink and roll
> hop and jump.

▶ Repeat these to form very simple movement motifs.

▶ Demonstrate clear, uncomplicated examples and repeat for others to learn the pattern and phrasing of the motif.

▶ Finish with a follow-my-leader game with the leader at the front or in the centre of the class and the rest facing and following the leader's motif.

KEY STAGE 2
Accompaniment: Action words and phrases

▶ Explore different ways of turning, stopping, rising and sinking.

▶ Create a short phrase of movement a *motif* that expresses:

> spin   grip   rise   fall

▶ Change the order of the words to form another motif.

▶ In pairs, perform each motif separately then learn each other's motifs.

▶ Create a dance where each motif is performed individually and then together in unison.

▶ Find more words/phrases to form the basis of new movement motifs, for example:

> stop — start — wobble — collapse
> go — freeze — go — wait — go — arrive
> hop, hop — jump — turn

▶ Walk to a steady beat – add a jump or a leap, a turn, and a gesture. The pathway can be straight or curved but the order of actions must remain the same.

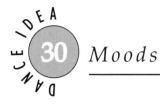

30 Moods

KEY STAGE 1

Accompaniment: Cartoon themes. Soundtrack from the Walt Disney cartoon *Snow White and the Seven Dwarfs*

Tell the story of *Snow White and the Seven Dwarfs*. Make up the dwarfs' names and create appropriate shapes and actions for them.

▶ Create a motif about *Angry* stamping and stomping.

▶ In contrast, create a motif about *Shy* tiptoeing tentatively with tiny steps forwards and backwards.

▶ Now, establish motifs for *Sneezy* using slowly stepping and sudden, percussive jumps and turns.

▶ Try making a motif for *Sleepy*, yawning, stretching and then sinking slowly to the floor.

▶ Lastly, encourage the children to improvise around and to create two short movement motifs based on opposite moods, for example, 'Happy' performing a jolly, hopping and jumping dance and 'Weepy' shuffling, sobbing and stopping.

KEY STAGE 2

Accompaniment: *Appalachian Spring* by Aaron Copeland

▶ Use slow, gentle, opening, closing and turning actions at high and low levels, possibly including some rolling and curling actions along the ground, to form one motif based on a slow, gentle, day-dreaming character.

▶ Create another motif which is quick, lively and exuberant in character. Jumps, hops, turns and isolated body parts moving percussively are suitable movement possibilities.

▶ Establish a strong, forceful, dominant motif using stamping, jumping, pushing and turning actions.

▶ Take one of the motifs and develop it with travelling actions and changes in direction to further develop the expression of the character.

► Work with a partner who has taken the same character for the dance and create a dance, possibly even with interchanging motifs.

► Alternatively, dance in threes, each with a separate motif to form an action and reaction dance.

► Consider dancing in unison as well as in opposition and moving at the same time together as well as one at a time.

Dancing in unision

31 Movement Conversations

KEY STAGE 1
No Accompaniment

Use contrasting travelling actions to form a simple movement motif, for example:

> stamping and stopping
> hopping and jumping
> skipping and turning.

► Perform the motif yourself and ask the class to follow you so that they learn your motif.

► Perform the motif yourself and ask the class to move after you in their own way, thus creating movement conversations.

KEY STAGE 2
No Accompaniment

► Improvise with the formation of a quick, strong jumping motif contrasted with a slow, light, turning phrase.

► Create a dance in pairs with dynamic contrasts evident. Make sure that each person has the opportunity to be light **and** strong.

► Explore moving together in unison, in opposition and in conversation. Do **not** mime. Speak through whole body actions and rhythms.

► Use the question and answer mode to make up a dance of many moods, based on a conversation through the multi-lingual language of dance – a language without words.

Movement conversations

32 Two's Company, Three's a Crowd

KEY STAGE 1

Accompaniment: *The Swan, The Royal March of the Lion, The Elephant – Carnival of the Animals* by Saint-Saens

Many very young children can dance together in pairs and small groups. The trio is the hardest formation for this age group to come to terms with.

▶ Try only very simple devices such as creating a shape, a diamond, a volcano and a star in threes. Practise growing slowly and shrinking quickly – repeat in reverse.

▶ Form lines in threes to form monsters, trains, animals and insects. Be aware of the child in the middle and regularly change leaders so that no one is 'the head', 'the body' or 'the tail' for too long.

Two's company, three's a crowd

▶ Explore moving on and off the spot in trio formations.

Accompaniment: *Aquarium, The Aviary, The Donkey – Carnival of the Animals* by Saint-Saens

▶ Create three separate movement motifs for three different characters:

> dreamy – opening, closing and turning
> excited – hopping, jumping and turning
> angry – stamping, stopping, shaking.

▶ Create groups of three and choose one motif each. Perform the individual motifs separately.

▶ Use the leader and follower and action and reaction relationships to form the basis of movement conversations. Improvise around the following:

> moving in unison
> shadow and mirroring
> echoing
> conversing two via one
> conversing one at a time.

▶ Choose two or three structures listed above and create a dance based on 'an eternal triangle'.

33 *Group Shapes and Formations*

Circles revolving

KEY STAGE 1

Accompaniment: contrasting nursery rhyme tunes for tiptoeing, skipping, marching, trotting and galloping

► The circle can revolve clockwise and anti-clockwise. It can expand and contract. It can rise and fall. Explore these possibilities in a class, then in a smaller group.

► Put two groups together, one inside the other, and explore what is possible with double circles and circles within circles.

► Create short group dances starting with a line and finishing in a line with a circle shape between the two lines.

KEY STAGE 2

Accompaniment: *The Entertainer* by Scott Joplin

► A line can start, travel, stop. Choose reliable leaders and explore starting and stopping as one group unit.

► Use a leader/follower formation to introduce varied and contrasting movement motifs, i.e. each leader has a new motif which the line learns and follows.

► Single files, double files and circles all have the potential for interweaving. Find ways of forming and re-forming lines and circles using the idea of interweaving.

► There are a variety of group shapes which can be formed. Some of these are irregular and some are regular such as:

blocks	triangles	zig-zags
lines	fans	spirals
circles		

Create a dance which highlights at least two of the group shapes listed above.

34 *Binary and Ternary Form*

Binary or A.B. form is a dance in two parts, which contrast with each other but are linked through the initial stimulus. It is essentially a simple short dance in two parts.

Ternary or A.B.A. form, consists of two contrasting sections, with the first being repeated immediately after the second. The A.B.A. dance form is probably one of the most commonly used choreographic forms because it appears to be balanced and logical. However, it is somewhat predictable and both teachers and dancers must bear in mind that rules are made to be broken.

KEY STAGE 1
Accompaniment: *Jack and Jill* (AB form); *Humpty dumpty* (ABA form); *The Grand Old Duke of York* (AB form); *Wee Willie Winkie* (ABA form)

▶ Use simple action phrases such as:
'I **am** happy! So **am** I!'
'Rain **falls** . . . Sun **shines**!'
'**I'm** big . . . **you're** small!'
to create very simple, unaccompanied dances in binary form (A.B.)

▶ Find a short piece of music in binary form and allow the children to react spontaneously to the rhythms and dynamics of each section.

▶ Play only part of the music (either the 'A' or 'B' section) and allow the music/sound to dictate the formation of motifs or phrases.

▶ Older infants can create dances which are short and simply structured, in ternary form (A.B.A.). This form is very useful for performance pieces and assemblies.

KEY STAGE 2
Accompaniment: piano rags – Scott Joplin; Slavonic dances – Dvořak; polkas, waltzes, marches – Strauss; piano pieces – Tchaikovsky

▶ Set and perform a task in binary form (A.B.). Develop the second part (B) from some fragment of movement contained in the first part (A).

▶ Individually, create two separate motifs for part (A) and part (B) of the A.B.A. structure.

▶ In groups of three develop and extend the A and B motifs. Use changes in body actions, dynamics, level, direction and size to make the A and B motifs into entire sections or parts of a section.

▶ Many popular classical pieces of music are written in A.B.A. form. Spend time listening to these and use the music as a stimulus for dance.

35 Rondo Form

The Rondo form is ABACADA and can be likened to a song which has contrasting verses interspersed by a repetitive chorus. The verses are quite different, but the structure provides security by returning to Section A, the chorus.

Old Macdonald's farm

KEY STAGE 1
Accompaniment: *Old Macdonald had a farm*

> *'Old Macdonald had a farm E I E I O*
> *And on that farm he had some . . .'*

▶ Clap the beat and stamp and stomp in and out of spaces to familiarise the children with the song.

▶ Before introducing the animals, which offer contrasts in action, level, speed and strength, work on the chorus with the farmer pulling on a huge pair of imaginary Wellington boots and a large straw hat, then

Each verse introduces a new animal

striding and stamping strong, flat feet. Make sure that the children can recognise and repeat the chorus before moving on. The chorus could be performed in one large class circle shape if more control is required.

▶ Each verse introduces a new animal, for example:

> chickens, scurrying round the farmyard
> rabbits, jumping through the fields
> pigs, rolling in sticky, squelchy mud
> birds, swooping, fluttering, hovering and settling
> horses, trotting and galloping.

▶ Practise the whole rhyme by inserting the chorus between the verses to form a dance in *Rondo* form.

Lord of the Dance

KEY STAGE 2

Accompaniment: take the hymn *The Lord of the Dance* and structure it into verses and a chorus

The chorus is the repetitive element in the dance and needs to be structured simply, for example:

'Dance, Dance, wherever you may be
(Turn, turn . . . run and stop)
I am the Lord of the Dance said he
(Rising and sinking actions)
And I'll lead you all wherever you may be
(Follow-my-leader lines)
And I'll lead you all in the dance said he . . .'
(Circle formations).

The verses are explicit in meaning, and older children may be able to find symbolic motifs to express the narrative.

 *Spiders*

Incy Wincy Spider

KEY STAGE 1

Accompaniment: *Incy Wincy Spider* rhyme

'Incy Wincy Spider climbed up the water spout
Down came the raindrops and washed poor Incy out,
Out came the sunshine and dried up all the rain
And Incy Wincy Spider climbed up the spout again.'

As a finger rhyme	Starting with fingers, climbing high in the air, then fluttering fingers, arms stretching wide and finally a repeat of the climbing fingers, finishing with hands reaching upwards.

As a whole body activity

Spiders	Slowly uncurling and stretching into wide, spindly, balanced shapes.
Climbing	Stepping slowly and silently on wide hands and feet.
Rain	Suddenly curling small on the floor, followed by rolling gently from side to side.
Sunshine	Slowly rising and stretching into wide, standing shapes with long necks and with faces looking upwards, followed by dancing from space to space with arms outstretched to represent the sunshine drying up the rain.
Up the spout again	Making wide shapes as before then scurrying quickly and lightly from place to place – finishing in a balanced 'spider' shape.

Anancy, the spider man

KEY STAGE 2

Accompaniment: The rhyming chants from the story

There are many stories about Anancy, the famous spider man of West African and Caribbean folk tales. Anancy was a spider, but he thought he was a man. He was little and lively and he always wanted everyone to think he was the best. He wanted to be the best looking, the cleverest, the bravest and the strongest. But how could this tiny spiderman be the strongest? Everyone thought he was a weakling!

Here Comes Anancy	Making spider shapes from low curled shapes with feet, hands and finger tips leading. Then stepping slowly from hand to hand and foot to foot.
Balancing on the high wire	On one, two or three body parts in stretched spidery shapes.

| Spinning a web | Try spinning on feet from high to low, on hands and feet round and round, then in tucked shapes on bottoms. |

One day Anancy decided to show everyone how strong he really was. He performed balancing tricks on the high wires of his spider's web, and he looked down on a crocodile in the river chanting:

> *'Anancy is brave, Anancy is strong*
> *Come on crocodile, come along!'*

Then he jumped down right under the crocodile's nose.

> *'You crazy, man?' says Alligator.*
> *'You wanna try?' says Anancy.*
> *'Let's have a tug of war!'*

| Anancy the acrobat | Use stepping and balancing actions into spaces, attempt acrobatic tricks using jumps, turns, cartwheels and balances on and off the high wire, as though teasing the crocodile. |

| Anancy the brave, Anancy the strong. It's a tug o' war, so come along! | Prancing and dancing on wide feet with stretched spidery arms. |

Suddenly he found himself balancing on a foot, a huge foot, an elephant's foot! Little Anancy, the brave spiderman looked up at the elephant and the elephant laughed.

> *'You crazy, man?' said the elephant.*
> *'Wanna try?' said Anancy.*

Anancy gave the elephant one end of the rope and the crocodile the other end. And they pulled and they pulled and they pulled. Each one of them thought that Anancy, the tiny spiderman, was at the other end.

| Tug-o-war | Stand in the centre of the room and divide the class in half with the elephants spaced out along one wall and the crocodiles spaced out along the opposite wall. Check the contrasting animal shapes, then point to each group in turn to produce pulling and staggering actions. Orchestrate the action so that the groups pull and stagger, towards and away from you in turn. Try this in groups of three with one child as |

Anancy and the others as elephant and crocodile.

The rope got tighter and tighter and Anancy performed clever balancing tricks on the 'high wire'. Elephant and crocodile pulled and pulled again until, at the same moment, the crocodile and elephant gave up.

All fall down!   Check the spacing, and alert the children before the final fall.

Anancy wins and dances away singing:

> *'Anancy the brave, Anancy the strong,*
> *Anancy is clever and brave and strong!'*

Clever little spider   Creeping to a space, then dancing with lots of
Clever little man!   different balancing and acrobatic actions
                                included in the dance. The elephant and
                                crocodile join in and follow Anancy in a follow-
                                my-leader line.

37 *Movement and Maths*

KEY STAGE 1

Accompaniment: Number chants, words, voice or percussive sounds

▶ Use the words: straight, spiky, flat, round, pointed and twisted to make different shapes. Can you tell which shape fits which words?

▶ Use the rhyme:

> *'As tall as a house*
> *As small as a mouse*
> *As wide as a gate*
> *As thin as a pin.'*

to find different shapes and sizes alone or with others. Once this rhyme is familiar, change the order of the lines so that the nature of the dance sequence changes. The children must listen, then move. Also, say the lines sometimes quickly, sometimes slowly, sometimes loudly, sometimes softly to change the speed and strength of actions.

▶ Draw a pattern on the floor. *Can you walk, then run, then skip this pattern?*

▶ Create simple chanting and counting phrases using stamping steps towards and away from you; starting with four steps forward, four steps back. Then, try jumping from side to side. Eventually a short sequence of jumping and stamping actions can be formed with the children counting out the numbers.

▶ Introduce number rhymes such as:

> *'One two, buckle my shoe,*
> *Three four, knock at the door,*
> *Five six, pick up sticks,*
> *Seven eight, lay them straight,*
> *Nine ten, a big fat hen.'*

> *'One potato, two potato, three potato, four,*
> *Five potato, six potato, seven potato more.'*

These games can be played traditionally or as an accompaniment to marching, stamping, hopping or jumping. Try using the hopscotch format of hopping and jumping in the 'potato' rhyme.

KEY STAGE 2
Accompaniment: Times table chants, recorded music featuring changes in speed and strength

▶ Create a times table dance which is easily remembered and can be repeated as the warm-up for several movement sessions. Try each table in turn and do not mix the tables within one dance. Try stamping, jumping, clapping to the beat, then introduce combinations such as hopping and jumping, clapping and stamping.

▶ Create a counting dance which involves stepping, jumping, hopping, skipping, stamping, trotting and galloping. The simple format of such a piece is indicated above in the times table dance.

▶ Take one straight, one curved and one zig-zag pathway and use these to form contrasting patterns on the floor.

▶ You are in a large box and can't get out . . . push all the surfaces slowly, then quickly. Explore the words – *above, below, sideways, forwards* and *backwards*. Finally find your own way out of the box.

▶ To long and short, loud and soft sounds, create a sequence of movement which contains contrasting curved and angular air patterns.

▶ In groups of three, make the shape of a triangle. Try to grow and shrink into this shape, and then to travel as a triangle together to a new space.

► A triangle is made up of three angles. What shape can you make if one person separates and the two remaining people make an angular shape? Try forming more of your own angular shapes together or individually.

► Use the whole class group plus some simple addition, subtraction and division sums to demonstrate maths in action. Multiplication is more difficult as you would need a cast of thousands for this!

Maths in action

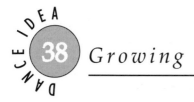 *Growing*

Springtime

KEY STAGE 1
Accompaniment: Ragamuffin 'Turn of the Tide'

Baby birds – Form a class circle to represent the shape of a bird's nest and develop a continuous sequence of bird-like activities: hatching on the spot; flapping wings in turn around the circle; hopping together in the same direction on one leg; hopping together in the opposite direction on the other leg; balancing and hopping on the spot; sinking low to rest.

Baby rabbits – Little bunny jumps on two feet with hands held high in front of chest. Big bunny jumps from two long, strong legs to two stretched arms.

Little lambs – Stretching on to hands and feet; stepping and balancing; gambolling (skipping) from space to space and falling.

Tadpoles – Explore through movement the lifecycle of the frog: make a class cluster of frogspawn by curling tightly in low, round shapes; slowly grow and wriggle to a space; wriggle high and low on the spot and then in and out of each other without touching; make frog-like shapes and finally leap along in one long, frog line from space to space.

Growing together

Things that grow

KEY STAGE 2
Accompaniment: *Voice sounds* (for balloons): *Soil Festivities* by Vangelis (for elastic and parachutes): *Nursery rhymes, sporting themes, percussive sounds* (for shoes)

▶ Blow up three different balloons (round, long and twisted) in stages and ask children to move in response. Let the air out of the balloon and ask for spontaneous reactions. Work individually and then in small groups.

- In pairs, use elastic to explore stretching and shrinking into different shapes and at contrasting levels.

- Use shoes to highlight the growth of people. Start with baby shoes accompanied by nursery rhyme tunes. Sporty music introduces trainers and exaggerated sporting skills. Other examples are trendy teenage shoes, ladies' high-heeled shoes, Wellington boots and dancing shoes.

- Start curled low beneath a huge piece of material or a parachute and grow together using a combination of staccato and flowing actions. Follow this with one sudden shrinking action.

- Create dances about other things that grow, such as eggs, bubble gum, rubbish tips, dirty washing.

Storms

The flood – Noah's Ark

KEY STAGE 1

Accompaniment: *Who built the ark?* (song): Saint-Saens *Carnival of the Animals: The Animals went in two by two* from *'Over and Over Again'* by Barbara Ireson and Christopher Rowe

- Build the ark using chopping, hammering and sawing actions in sitting, kneeling or standing shapes. Play rhythmic percussion to emphasise exaggerated actions and sing *Who built the ark? Noah, Noah? Who built the Ark? Brother Noah built the ark.*

- Use Saint-Saens' *Carnival of the Animals* to explore different types of animal, for example:

> the lion – prowling proudly
> chickens – pecking and shuffling
> tortoises – slowly inching along
> fish – weaving freely
> elephants – plodding
> swans – floating and gliding.

- Introduce animal categories and explore in dance which animals are:

> creeping, crawling creatures
> prowling, growling creatures

tiny, furry creatures
enormous, hairy creatures
slippery, sliding creatures.

▶ Use the song *The Animals Went in Two by Two*, to explore pair work in leader, follower and side by side relationships.

▶ Create a storm with raindrop fingers and feet, flickering, tapping, clapping and running from space to space. Introduce thunder turning and rolling and lightning leaping spikily.

▶ Finish the dance in a follow-my-leader line led by the dove (a child) and Noah (the teacher). The raven (a child) is at the back of the line and disappears before the class forms a final celebration circle.

▶ Make a circle dance where all the above activities happen within and around the circle.

▶ Create rain dances using rhymes and rituals. Introduce the *rain cycle*, *puddles* and *circles* as stimuli for dance.

Shipwreck!

KEY STAGE 2

Accompaniment: Sea shanties; voice and percussive sounds; the sailors' hornpipe and hand-held percussion

Getting Ready – loading cargo in lines, scrubbing decks, hoisting sails, heaving ropes.

Salute the Captain – getting ready actions interrupted by arrival of captain as in 'port and starboard' game.

Setting Sail – follow-my-leader lines, pull up the anchors and make group boat shapes swaying rhythmically.

Sailors' Hornpipe – the sailors dance for each other to keep fit, skipping with arms folded and elbows high, incorporating hoisting sails, pulling up the anchor and heaving ropes.

The Storm – high crashing waves rising, falling, advancing and

Salute the captain

114

retreating. Sea spray runs and stops and changes direction suddenly. Whirlpools spiral high and low and wind, rain and thunder run – fall – roll – jump.

Abandon Ship! – using combinations of sway, balance, fall, rise, roll and jump, create sequences of sailors falling from ships into the ocean.

Saved! – small groups huddle together in lifeboats, rowing rhythmically whilst chanting:

> *'Row row row the boats*
> *Safely to the shore,*
> *Merrily, merrily, merrily, merrily,*
> *safely to the shore.'*

Celebration dances – groups create circle dances using hornpipe steps and other actions in clockwise and anti-clockwise directions and in and out of the circle.

Make a dance in narrative form. Start with 'Getting Ready' and finish with 'Celebration Dances'.

▶ Use pirate stories as the starting point for dance activities.

▶ Develop the theme to include other natural disasters such as earthquakes, tidal waves and volcanoes.

40 Beasts

Mini-beasts

KEY STAGE 1
Accompaniment: *Soil Festivities* by Vangelis

Explore:

Ant movements – protective queen, guarding soldier ants and scurrying workers fetching food.

Worm movements – sliding and slithering; burrowing in and out of the soil.

Spider movements – creeping, spinning webs on spot and creeping again.

Centipede movements – follow-my-leader line exploring the space in circles, spirals and figures of eight.

Create habitats for different types of mini-beasts in large and small class groups, for example, The Beehive, The Web, An Ant Hill, A Wormery and even a Butterfly Farm. (You could make a dance about the life cycle of a butterfly.)

Make a dance using the above elements – the music may suggest certain mini-beasts.

'Big beasts'

KEY STAGE 2

Accompaniment: *Wooloomooloo* by J. M. Jarré: *The Big Beasts Boogie* by L. T. Davies

Evolution – dinosaurs emerging from eggs or dinosaurs emerging from the water.

Moving on to land – struggling, scrambling, crawling, pushing, pulling, on different parts, on all fours.

Moving on land – unfolding oddly or beautifully shaped plants and trees, animals moving with giant strides, lumbering and stumbling.

Make-believe monsters

Big beasts – Diplodocus, Brontosaurus, lines of four to six working as one with strong, rhythmical stepping.

Spiky beasts – Triceratops, Stegosaurus, working individually growing spiky shapes on heads or backs – sharp, jerky movements.

Flying reptiles – Pterosaurs; smooth, light gliding movements; opening, closing and turning. Wings working from centre of body.

Water monsters – Ichthyosaurs, Plesiosaurs during movements – swooping and running, 'body waves' rippling through the spine.

▶ Make a dance which creates a landscape for the dinosaurs to explore – through jungles, across deserts, over mountains, into water.

▶ Introduce make-believe monsters through poems and stories such as *Jabberwocky* by C. S. Lewis and the story of the Chinese Dragon Monster.

▶ Use the song and dance – *The Big Beasts Boogie* by L. T. Davies, to create a light-hearted dance about dinosaurs.

41 *Snow*

Jack Frost

KEY STAGE 1

Accompaniment: Tchaikovsky's *Concerto No 1 in B Flat Major. The Snowman* by Raymond Briggs, music by Howard Blake

The snowflakes run with quick, quiet feet in and out of all the spaces, turning, swirling, sinking and rising as they cover the floor with a carpet of snow.

Jumping, jerky Jack Frosts enter. With icy, spiky fingers and toes and jagged knees and elbows, tiptoeing, darting and jumping high and low with 'frozen' pauses in between each action.

Ice patterns are formed by making wide, stretched shapes on the floor; long, thin icicle shapes and icy, spiky shapes standing.

Use the idea of Jack Frost turning everything he touches to ice by playing the *Jack Frost Game*. Choose one person to be Jack Frost moving freely in any spiky, jagged way. That person moves from space to space touching others who then freeze in an icy shape. When everyone is frozen, on a given signal everyone melts to the ground.

▶ Create footprints in the snow, of Jack Frost, a snowman, birds, animals and people. Make follow-my-leader prints.

▶ Play snow games – skating upon frozen snow, gliding, swirling, balancing and turning quickly. Throw, catch and roll snowballs.

Ice skater

▶ Use the story of *The Snowman*, R. Briggs and H. Blake, to create another snow based story.

Polar regions

KEY STAGE 2
Accompaniment: *The Snow is Dancing* by Debussy. *Tubular Bells* by Mike Oldfield

It's snowing – an imaginary exploration of the polar terrain; running and stopping in different directions at high and low levels.

The snow is getting deeper – slow, strong stamping steps with high knees and feet pulling away from the ground (snowprints).

It's getting colder – shivering and shaking up high, down low, on the spot and in and out of spaces.

It's freezing – shrinking small then growing into spiky, icy shapes.

Ice floes – jumping from ice floe to ice floe – careful the sea is cold! Jump and balance, face another direction to jump to another ice floe.

Glaciers – moving slowly and carefully along straight lines, making slipping, balancing and falling movements.

Climbing a snowy mountain – on the spot climbing actions, balancing across a knife edge mountain ridge.

Icebergs – small group shapes moving carefully!

Make a number of short episodic dance pieces by:

▶ using drawings, photos and poems about snow, for example, *The Snowflake* by Walter de la Mare to illuminate the images of snow

▶ introducing the animals which live in polar regions – polar bears, penguins, walruses and reindeer and make the shapes and actions of these animals

▶ creating action-packed confrontations between man and nature in the polar regions – use advancing and retreating and circling actions.

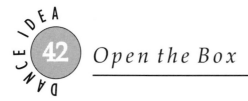

42 Open the Box

Small boxes, big boxes, shoe boxes, prop boxes and even round hat boxes can trigger off a range of imaginative and inventive movement and dance activities.

Boxes

KEY STAGE 1

Accompaniment: Nursery songs. Music from popular cartoons and advertisements

Jack-in-the-box – this traditional toy creates an element of surprise with his sudden appearing and disappearing acts. Use a woodblock or castanets to indicate the high jumps when the box opens. Contrast slow, sinking actions with sudden jumps. Soon the children will be able to time their own sequences.

Jack-in-the-box

Musical boxes – imagine a musical box which plays a different tune each time the lid is lifted! It could start with a march and follow with the rhythm of skipping, jumping, trotting, galloping and stepping actions. This activity can be repeated many times. Try to catch the class out by playing the excerpts in a different order.

Shoe boxes – bring a collection of boots and shoes and supplement these with others cut from magazines. Create imaginary characters to wear the shoes and explore all the different ways these might move, for example, high heels (*tiptoeing and tottering*), hobnail boots (*stamping and marching*), flippers (*waddling and flapping*), slippers (*shuffling*), Wellingtons (*stomping and wading*). Other interesting footwear includes ice/roller skates, riding boots, clown shoes, baby shoes and giant shoes.

▶ Extend the shoe box idea to hat boxes, for example, builder's helmet (*digging, drilling, painting and hammering*), jockey's cap (*walking, trotting, galloping*), a chef's hat (*stirring, shaking, tossing*), uniform hats such as a soldier, a policeman and a firefighter and last but not least, a cowboy hat.

▶ Create a dance based on the ideas about and linked together by the 'box' theme. Add a dressing up box and its contents to the action.

The prop box

KEY STAGE 2

Accompaniment: Musical comedy, for example, music cartoons, silent movies: popular musicals: *Barnum, Cats, Les Miserables* by Andrew Lloyd Webber

The contents of the prop box are many and varied, select one from the list below:

hat	bucket
shoe	gown
shawl	cloak
ball	wand
rope	flowers
newspaper	

Create a short dance motif using this property to dance with.

Imagine that you are trapped inside a huge wicker properties box. Find your way out. Explore the six-sided nature of the box using slow pushing actions in different directions. What happens when you get out?

▶ Extend the idea of the shoe and the hat box (from Key Stage 1) in groups of three. Each choose a different pair of shoes or a different hat and form a dance where three characters meet, part, lead, follow, act and react with each other. Attempt to make this into a dance comedy in cartoon-type fashion.

▶ Create a 'box of delights'. The contents of this box are a mystery and the children can transform themselves into almost anything. The 'box of delights' contains items which can be used as clues, for example:

> a globe – takes you into far and distant lands
> a spacecraft – creates new worlds in the future
> a broom – denotes hard work
> a wand – takes you into a magical, mystery land.

▶ Create a dance in small groups called 'The Box of Delights' and based on the use of at least two and not more than five props.

Rain

It's raining

KEY STAGE 1

Accompaniment: *John Had Great Big Waterproof Boots On* (A.A. Milne) by Silver Burdett/H. Fraser Simpson

▶ Explore the popular rain rhymes such as 'It's raining it's pouring'; 'Rain, rain go away' and 'Pitter, patter, raindrops'.

▶ Try out phrases like *drip – drop – splosh* and *pitter, patter, gurgle – splash* to form short sequences about the rain.

▶ *Puddles, puddles . . . everywhere!* Using one finger, then one toe to draw the puddle and then tiptoeing around; running round the other way and jumping in and out of puddles.

▶ Follow-my-leader raindrops. With light, then louder feet in pairs, in a class line and in a giant puddle-shaped circle.

▶ Create a dance in verse and chorus form (Rondo) with Verse 1 being the raindrops; Verse 2 being dressing up for rainy weather in Wellington boots, hats and mackintoshes; Verse 3 being the puddle dance; and the chorus being one of the rain rhymes suggested above.

Water music

KEY STAGE 2

Accompaniment: Voice and body sounds. Enya's *Watermark* album; Gene Kelly's *Singing in the Rain*; *Incantations* by Incantation

There are many aspects of rainfall which affect us. Explore the following:

▶ Percussive body sounds and actions which create a rainstorm effect. One child may like to lead all the sounds and action. Take turns.

▶ Create a free splashing dance. Encourage lots of foot and leg work, partners dancing around each other.

▶ Use Enya's *Watermark* music, with its evocative sounds, to improvise and create to.

▶ Create a four section dance piece around the rain cycle:
Evaporation, Elevation, Condensation and Precipitation.

▶ An umbrella is an extremely versatile prop to work with, dancing
around, under, over and turning with the umbrella. Create a dance to
the song *Singing in the Rain* using an umbrella.

▶ With imaginary or real umbrellas create the rainbow behind which the
sun might appear, perhaps in canon form, one after the other.

▶ Use the Rainforest as a starting point to a dance:

> The Rainstorm
> Forest Peoples
> The Balance of Nature
> Celebrations.

44 *Festivals of Light*

There are many festivals of light which happen at different points in the
year throughout the world. Celebrations such as Christmas, Chanukah
(Jewish), St Lucia (Christian/Swedish) and Diwali (Hindu) to name but a
few. Most festivals of light involve candles, but some also include
fireworks and 'fairy' lights.

Celebrations

KEY STAGE 1
Accompaniment: Silence or suitable recorded music: festival songs
around the world

▶ Create a procession of imaginary candle lights. Walk slowly and
carefully with palms held upwards as though holding a precious light.

▶ Lead, or choose a child to lead, a leader/follower formation in a line
and then a circle.

▶ Create a circle dance which focuses on going towards and away from
the centre point of the circle. Try travelling together sideways around
the outside of the circle.

Circle celebrations

▶ The giving and receiving of gifts is often very much a part of the festivals of light. Refer to the *dance idea* on 'Boxes' and add gift boxes to the list of possibilities. Ask the children to dance about *what's inside the box*.

▶ Try to find pieces of music which are suitable for the festivals of light explored in this *dance idea*.

Christmas

KEY STAGE 2
Accompaniment: Christmas carols; Pachelbel's *Canon*; *The First Christmas*, (poem by T.S. Eliot); Charpentier's *Midnight Mass for Christmas Eve*

▶ After reading and researching the several different versions of the nativity story create a group dance in A.B.A. form.

▶ Make a dance with Sections A and C in tableaux form and Section C moving and dancing.

▶ Work on movement and stillness by practising how to come out of and get back into a tableaux shape. Start by giving the class 'set' tableaux shapes such as Mary and Joseph on their journey to Bethlehem. The idea of the *hold* shot on a video which moves before and after the action is a good way of explaining the tableaux movement concept to children. The tableaux include:

> The journey to Bethlehem
> The stable scene
> The shepherd scene
> The three kings
> The journey away from Bethlehem.

Movements should link each of these scenes.

▶ In Section B, create a dance of praise with more complex pathways of processing lights – exploring curves, arcs, circles, spirals and figures of eight. Small groups may process to form a kaleidoscope of patterns. Suitable accompaniment might be the Exultant and Gloria from, for example, Charpentier's Mass.

A dance of praise

▶ *The Three Kings* by H. W. Longfellow lends itself to exploring rhythm within a narrative supported by movement.

45 The Wizard of Oz

Create a dance drama, for performance, in narrative dance form based on the story *The Wizard of Oz* by L. Frank Baum.

KEY STAGE 1

Accompaniment: from the musical *The Wonderful Wizard of Oz* by E. Harburg and H. Arlen (starring Judy Garland)

▶ Work on magic beginnings and endings with the wind whirling, thunder rolling, lightning flashing. Form a class group 'rainbow shape' and travel under it yourself to represent going 'over the rainbow'. Eventually one child will take your place in the final performance piece but *not yet!* – everyone at this stage takes part in everything!

The Wizard of Oz

► Follow the Yellow Brick Road with simple follow-my-leader formations which travel in different ways. Work on a variety of step patterns and eventually put the children into threes with each having the opportunity to lead and follow the action.

► Three characters – the Scarecrow, the Tin Man and the Cowardly Lion. Make each shape, and discover different ways to move in turn. Start with the Scarecrow, with long, dangling arms and flippy, floppy head. Use the 'Dingle Dangle Scarecrow' poem to colour this character.

The Tin Man makes robot actions with his stiff, jointed body and a jerky, jolting dance.

The Cowardly Lion is like a large cat creeping towards and away from the teacher. Add leaps, rising, sinking and roaring.

► The City of Oz is a magical and mysterious place. There are many streets, alleyways and passages which lead towards the Wizard. Try creeping under, squeezing through, clambering over and stepping around imaginary obstacles. Act, in role, as the Wizard of Oz. The children approach you and retreat from you first as the Scarecrow, then as the Lion and finally as the Tin Man. Create dance phrases for the Wizard using slow rising and turning, sudden spiky fingers and explosive jumps.

KEY STAGE 2
Accompaniment: From the musical *The Wonderful Wizard of Oz* by E. Harburg and H. Arlen

► The whirlwind – use voice sounds and action words, for example, whoosh, swoosh, ssh, whee, whirl, curl, flash and fly to accompany the whirlwind which carries Dorothy in a spiral from earth into another world.

► The Yellow Brick Road – try skipping, stepping, marching, trotting, hopping and jumping along the Yellow Brick Road. Change leaders frequently and include simple step patterns which everyone else can copy. Use the idea of *magic shoes* to develop contrasting step patterns. Experiment with different ways of travelling along the Yellow Brick Road tentatively, fearfully, boldly, happily, sadly. Develop this in pairs and then in groups of four.

Use the song from the film to accompany a rhythmic song and dance routine.

► The three characters – spend time introducing the shapes and exploring the ways in which each of the characters move. Use visual images to create a scatty Scarecrow, a 'deadpan', heartless Tin Man and a Cowardly Lion. Refer to *Key Stage 1* for the movement characteristics of each one.

► Work on the journey to the magical City of Oz. Use the images of castles, passageways, haunted houses, castles, dungeons and steep stairways to create hazards. Create a huge, action-packed disturbance both in sound and in movement to represent the Wizard of Oz.

Finish the dance with a series of amazing 'appearing' and 'disappearing' acts.

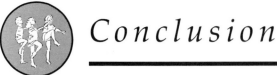 # *Conclusion*

'Dance is a distinct art form, with its own history, body of knowledge, aesthetic values, cultural contexts and artistic products. It offers a variety of learning opportunities and enables participants to enjoy physical experiences as well as develop intellectual sensibilities. Pupils can understand themselves and others by learning in and through dance. Dance also provides particular opportunities for cross-curricular work.'

(National Curriculum Interim Report, PE Working Group, Feb 1991)

Let's Dance is the result of dancework produced in collaboration with classroom teachers, specialist and primary advisers. It has evolved in response to the statement made by Angela Rumbold as Minister of Education in March 1989:

'We attach great importance to the study of dance in schools. We recognise that dance makes a unique contribution to the educational process.'

In April 1992, the final order for Physical Education for England and Wales was published which made dance a statutory part of the curriculum at Key Stages 1 and 2. The inclusion of dance in the National Curriculum means that for all children in primary schools this elemental form of human expression becomes a required part of a broad and balanced education.

Let's Dance has been written as a resource to support teachers working at Key Stages 1 and 2. It assumes no prior knowledge of dance or creative movement and contains some of the theory and much of the practice which generalist teachers frequently request.

Its aim is to provide a series of dance ideas which can be used, added to, and appraised according to needs and circumstances to build up into a simple, structured movement and dance course.